Possible Origins

A Cultural History of Chinese
Martial Arts, Theater and Religion

Possible Origins

A Cultural History of Chinese
Martial Arts, Theater and Religion

Scott Park Phillips

Youtube Channel: Youtube.com/c/NorthStarMartialArtsUSA

ISBN 13: 978-0692749012
ISBN 10: 0692749012

First Print Edition August 2016

Also available as an ebook

Cover: Actor in the role of Guan Gong holding a halberd, ~1920. May's Photo, California. From the Wylie Wong collection (who rescued this image in the trash). Courtesy of the Museum of Performance + Design.

Dedication

*To all those people in my life who have dedicated
themselves to meritorious action.*

Table of Contents

Consequences and Conclusions   171

Appendixes   183

Glossary   189

Bibliography   193

List of Illustrations

Introduction: Notes on Myself

The Origin of Chinese Martial Arts Matters

Penetrating heaven and pulverizing stones!

The phrase quoted above from Nobel Prize winner Mo Yan,[1] whose pen name means "don't speak," describes the power of the small cymbal used in Chinese opera to invoke martial prowess. It is imagination mixed with the power of martial arts practice—finely tuned metal ringing out into infinity. It is both a demand that we see things as they actually are, and a passionate request that we not constrain what is real by linking it to a narrow view.

This book is that cymbal. If you practice martial arts, I want to feed your enthusiasm. I want to offer the biggest, broadest view of the arts possible. I want to empower you to ask insightful questions which reveal hidden treasures and provoke innovation. My goal is to inspire vigorous, imaginative vision rooted in practice. I want you to hit that cymbal.

The more broadly we conceptualize the arts, the more potential there is for innovation. The result of being cut off from the historic and cultural roots of our arts is a poor and narrow vision. Of course, new roots can be invented, and that is a positive option many people take, but I will show that the original roots are still accessible, just waiting to be discovered—why not look at them? A broad understanding of the history and culture of Chinese martial arts will improve both access and innovation.

There is nothing to fear here; even if it eventually turns out that everything I say in this book is wrong, the journey is worthwhile. As it

1   Mo Yan, *Life and Death are Wearing Me Out*. Translated by Howard Goldblatt. New York: Arcade Pub., 2008.

stands, many people have a degree of dissatisfaction because the story they have about the origins of martial arts they practice is weak, or contradictory, or simply mythic. Even if the story I tell eventually ends up being discarded, practitioners will be better off for having considered it.

A part of this book is destructive. It is like a crowbar opening up the warped box that has been trying to contain martial arts for the last hundred years or so. Some of my work is easy: I'm simply revealing what has always been there but which is rarely acknowledged. Other parts of the book are creative, my best guesses as to how all these bits fit together. And still other parts are well-founded arguments based on historical and anthropological research. Ultimately the value of this work is in the hands of my readers—in the conversations and experiments you instigate.

So why is this guy wearing a tiger suit? *(figure 1)*. Is he attending some kind of battlefield pajama party? Is this an outdated type of battlefield attire similar to the big, black, fluffy hats the guards at Buckingham Palace wear? Does he even do martial arts?

When it comes to the history of martial arts, my goal is to soften the certainties and sharpen the possibilities. Stories about the origins of martial arts are mostly square pegs in round holes. Some of these round pegs are small enough that with a bit of aggression they can be made to fit in square holes, but this does require taking off their edges.

The first problem is that the subject of martial arts has been mislabeled—a situation also faced by Mark Meulenbeld in writing his recent book *Demonic Warfare (2015)*. While studying Chinese fiction from a few hundred years ago, Meulenbeld discovered that the very notion of fiction is a modern invention. The actual subject is a unified whole that includes religion, ritualized militia organizations, and narratives of history, magic, and performing arts. My premise, which I arrived at very gradually, is similar: Martial arts, theater and religion were a single subject. Meulenbeld is an expert at interpreting historic texts; my authority comes from the somatic experience of practice—that is, doing martial arts, religion, dance, and theater.

It is challenging to find the right metaphors for reassembling something which was originally whole but is now separate: A broken-up rock, with pieces missing? A bridge between different realms? A bowl of soup made up of distinct ingredients? A square peg in a round hole?

Figure 1. Drawing by William Alexander, from *The Costume of China, Illustrated in forty-eight coloured engravings,* published in London in 1805. Courtesy of Wikimedia Commons.

Family members separated by time? A place obscured by darkness? An elephant felt by a blind man? None of these metaphors are quite right.

Let's take the metaphor of a rock: it has been broken into distinct pieces, some of which are lost, some of which have been separated long enough to grow moss. I haven't completely solved the puzzle of putting that rock back together, but I have enough of the pieces to see that it was once a whole. Still, there are unknowns. When I'm not sure where a piece fits, I make an educated guess.

The evidence in this book comes from many sources: historical, anthropological, religious, and conceptual. But the core of the evidence comes from my interactions with other practitioners. These include children I have taught and master artists I have studied with—from every continent, not just China.

I hope readers do not misunderstand me by supposing that I am diminishing the value of the martial arts by claiming that they are simultaneously performing arts. I am not doing that. The earliest film of jujitsu ever made shows a man in a dress suit and hat being attacked multiple times in various ways; he tosses, and disarms, his assailant over and over. It is highly theatrical, demonstrating that the first thing martial artists did when the camera was put on them was to create a script and a theatrical routine—as if to say, this is what fights should look like in the movies. Their first choice was to go theatrical. But the techniques are real; these guys were undeniably teaching functional martial skills. The martial lineages I inherited were transmitted by tough guys—probably mean, and certainly violent. Martial skills are found in dance and performance all over the world. There is a reason for the English expression, "Waltz him out the door." The down-up-up swirling momentum of the waltz is an effective method for removing a badly behaved person from a room—it is a martial skill.

This book is aimed at people who practice. Readers who want to go deeper will find a substantial list of references at the end, including my own published research. This book is about the big picture.

In this book I take for granted the notion that ritual is a core human experience. Ritual and ritualization are what makes us individuals, what gives us a feeling of belonging, what makes us insiders or outsiders. We do not just appear fully formed. Martial arts comprise a ritual tradition, and if you practice, you belong to that tradition—you own it. Is there any other ritual that has been exported from one culture to another as effectively as Asian martial arts have? That poses a related question: why be devoted to the rituals of another culture? What is the appeal? Clearly, many people try to reject the ritual elements of martial arts, but for the most part, in their rejection they merely end up modifying these rituals. Why is that? What is it about martial arts as ritual that allows it to so potently transcend the usual limitation of culture?

The idea that martial arts need to become *more real* is a kind of obsession, often blind to the value of traditional cultural contexts. There is an endless stream of ignorant complaints about the martial-arts world: it is too showy, too mystical, too religious, too brutal, too sweet, too weak, too magical, too difficult, too mean, too old, too comic, too crazy, too nice, too boring, and too greedy. Enough already! Let's address these complaints by putting the arts into a historic and cultural context so that we can judge them as they were created to be. We will never be very good at preserving or improving the arts if we don't have honest information about why and how they were created.

As practitioners, we are able to think about, and re-think, the way we train; to ask better questions and create better experiments. After all, the value of a ritual tradition will certainly be lost without creative adaptation.

The Need for a Book

Most of this book is *not* about me. I will tell my story by way of introduction, however, because the basis for my authority is not obvious at first glance. As I share the questions that have arisen in the course of my studies, from the people I have met, and from the experiences I've had, you may come to trust me, fear me, or decide I'm a clown. I do my best to offer my story without pretense.

What is my martial-arts experience? And how did I get so deep into it?
My father's father Wendell Phillips was a Rabbi, and an anthropologist, who traveled to every country on earth, and lived naked on an island off the coast of Singapore for ten years. My father's mother Alice Phillips was a political activist, and a master of rhetoric, who taught history and literature. I come from a family where I was expected to spend a lot of my time thinking and investigating. In the 1990s I volunteered to be a reader for my father's NPR radio show *Social Thought*, which ran for ten

years. This gave me, in effect, an unconventional graduate education in the history of ideas.

My father Michael Phillips was hippie royalty; people knew him as the guru of hippie money, business, and free love. Around 1971, he began going to Japan every year to "spend time thinking." He was closely connected to the San Francisco Zen Center, and when I was ten, instead of sending me away to summer camp, he sent me to the secluded Green Gulch Zen Monastery north of the city. I was its youngest adept. I worked in the kitchen, the fields, and on countless fun projects. There was sitting meditation twice a day and chanting at meals. In those days the monastery was a sexual paradise, and Zen students were always hooking up and asking to borrow my room. (Being the son of hippie royalty, I had been given the only room with a bath.)

I started learning Northern Shaolin from Bing Gong, a student of Kuo Lien-ying, in 1977, in a park in the Haight-Ashbury of San Francisco. I was ten years old. It was the center of everything hippie. Most of the adults in the park with me were learning *taijiquan*, which was understood to be *not very well understood*. It was seen as a way to access the mystical flow. As in, *go with the flow*. Bruce Lee was a fellow hippie, in our eyes, who spoke the same East-West philosophical language as Allan Watts, another hippie icon.

Hippies took easily to magical language, like the word qi, and shared stories about *kongling*, the ability to blast people with energy, sending them flying without even touching them. The martial arts world I entered had both outsider appeal and shared dreams.

Because I was introduced to martial arts through hippies, I saw the iconic little old man practicing *taijiquan* as part of the hippie movement. But I also knew that Chinese gangsters practiced kung fu. One day, the undercover police at my urban middle school all disappeared midday. The next day we learned why: a *tong* (Triad) gang called the Wai Ching had machine-gunned forty people in a restaurant in Chinatown, killing off the leadership of another *tong* called the Jo-Boys. It was the stuff of kung-fu movies, but it was real, and close to home. My friends and I had met young people in *tongs* because we had been to Chinatown to buy illegal fireworks from them. This part of the martial arts world was never far away.

My teacher, Bing Gong, had an aura: Chinese-American, hippie and Zen, with a shaved head—he appeared ageless to me. His Northern Shaolin skills, along with his perfect deportment, work ethic, and performing prowess, were legendary. In addition to Northern Shaolin,

Bing Gong taught me Guanping Yang style *taijiquan* and *yiquan*; I also had opportunities to perform with him. The core of *yiquan* training is *zhanzhuang* (standing still); all these years later, I am still greeting every sunrise with an hour of stillness.

What I thought martial arts were about, was going to change, and then change again, and then change again. *Claims would become contradictions.* Bing eventually introduced me to a new teacher, George Xu. On our first meeting, George Xu went into a diatribe against what he called "tofu tai chi." *You know,* the weak, flimsy stuff you can smash with a single heavy chop! George Xu was a recent immigrant from Shanghai. He had dark stories of the Cultural Revolution to tell, his own intimate experiences of violence. *Taijiquan* (Chen style) now became a serious fighting art that took hours of daily practice to even glimpse. He insisted I give up being a vegetarian if I expected to make progress.

I still remember the shock I got when George Xu said, "Your punches have no power. Why even bother to punch if your punches won't break bones?" At that point I was doing movement training eight hours a day, every day—much of it in dance—but it had never occurred to me that my punches should have the power to break bones. I had simply never thought about it.

The material George Xu taught wasn't fundamentally different from what I had learned before, as it built on the same solid foundation—it was the attitude that was different. George Xu was training my *yi*, the fighting intent of my movement. Every sweep, kick, strike, throw, grab, and joint lock had to be made real.

George Xu also taught *lanshouquan*, a type of Shaolin which was considered a mixture of internal and external skills; *liuhexinyi*, an internal martial art based on the movements of ten animals which, before the Communist revolution (1949), had only been taught to Muslims; *baguazhang*, an internal martial art based on walking in circles; and *baxian*, an internal system based on the *Eight Immortals* that was used for teaching sword forms. He was single-minded about training martial arts, and his genius in this regard cannot be overstated. He took us through the *Taijiquan Classics* line by line as a tool for analyzing our movement. Occasionally he would sit us down for a six-hour marathon translation of martial-arts writings such as those of Wang Xiangzai, a major innovator of the 1930s and the creator of *yiquan*.

At about this time a thing called *qigong* appeared on the scene. Modern American medicine was in disarray at the height of the AIDS/HIV epidemic, and that, along with lingering hippie nostalgia, created the perfect conditions for the explosion of "alternative" medicine. Suddenly every martial arts teacher was teaching *qigong*, and San Francisco was swamped by the arrival of new immigrants from mainland China calling themselves *qigong* masters.

Not only were the basic warmups I learned as a ten year old (which, as I would later learn, are shared by the Beijing Opera) now called *qigong*, but so was everything martial artists did. Now martial artists had a new career option: *healer*. In the 1990s people were seeking out martial artists to heal every ailment under the sun. *Qigong* was a panacea that could be used to cure anything. And all martial arts, but especially *taijiquan*, were framed as healing systems that were scientifically embedded with Traditional Chinese Medicine (TCM). *Qigong* was a catchall for everything from *kongling* (empty-force powers) to mind-reading to distance healing to psychic surgery. I was a skeptic. I had seen magic shows, faith healing, and circus routines; the fact that these magicians were now called "*qigong* masters" wasn't enough to convince me that this stuff was anything other than parlor tricks. Yet, I had my own experience of using *yiquan* standing postures to heal the constant flow of injuries I was getting. (Ironically; most of my injuries were from dance, not martial arts.) And my health *was* good, so I thought there might be something to the healing powers of *qigong*.

Something wasn't right, but it was years before David Palmer's book, *Qigong Fever* (2007), explained that after the end of the Cultural Revolution (1967–77) there was a big opening in mainland Chinese society that allowed everything religious and magical that had been suppressed for more than a generation to be practiced under the name *qigong*; and at the same time, a clique of Party officials protected *qigong* masters from public rebuke. The flow of *qigong* masters into the United States dropped off after an internal change in the Chinese Communist Party triggered a crackdown on "*qigong* cults" like Falun Gong, and followed it with executions and imprisonment. But that box had been opened, and the ideas about healing that came out of it could not be put back in.

George Xu brought several teachers over from China for us to study with; notably Zhang Xuixin, who taught Chen style *taijiquan*; and Ye Xiaolong, who taught *lanshouquan* and push hands. I learned a great deal from both of them. George Xu gave me professional training and set an example; he had, and still has, an insatiable appetite for learning.

After six years, of three to five hours a day, six days a week, with George Xu, I started studying with Bruce Kumar Franztis, whose *baguazhang* was exquisite. Franztis, who had lived in China, brilliantly delineated the differences between training the internal martial arts of *taijiquan, xingyiquan, baguazhang,* for fighting on the one hand, and *qigong* for health on the other. And he did it in a way that bound healing and fighting together as a unified practice. He worked out a vocabulary that set what we were doing apart from what we called "hucksterism." He also insisted that these arts came from Daoism and were part of an enlightenment tradition.

I am immensely grateful for what I learned from Franztis, yet his healing lessons often came with a righteousness that was inappropriately aggressive. Over the years, I have encountered this forceful approach to healing in many other practitioners, too. I have witnessed practitioners shouting things like, "This movement is *good* for your kidneys!" It turns out that this aggressiveness is a characteristic of Chinese modernity, not tradition.

In search of greater depth, I embarked on what became a nine year long apprenticeship in religious Daoism with Liu Ming, whose birth name was Charles Belyea. He was a long time practitioner of Tibetan Buddhism, a translator for visiting monks, and a founder of the Five Branches School of Traditional Chinese Medicine in Santa Cruz; he was also an amazing cook. While studying in Taiwan he met a Daoist hermit who initiated him into a family tradition of Orthodox Daoism (Zhengyidao).

Liu Ming was a serious scholar, and during that period I read enough about Daoism, Chinese religion, and Chinese history to earn an informal degree. My relationship to Liu Ming was close, and for the first few years, every time I left his house it was with a pile of his books or a long reading list. The next time I saw him, we would play intellectual ping-pong with the ideas in those books and I would leave with another pile. I practiced what he taught me with daily discipline: *daoyin*—a bit like yoga but with a lot of slapping, self-massage, rolling, banging, and flopping on the floor; *zuowang* sitting meditation—literally *sitting and forgetting*; and *jindan*, the "golden elixir," a ritual visualization practice. I also studied many Daoist scriptures, *fengshui*, aesthetics, and an array of calendrical, dietary, bathing, movement, and dream practices.

Rather than fitting nicely together, everything started to fall apart at that point. The more I learned about Daoism, Buddhism, and Confucianism, the less I saw a connection to martial arts. As counterintuitive as it sounds, I had to discard all my false assumptions before I could start seeing how these things fit together.

Toward the end of the 1990s, the popular rap group Wu Tang Clan's enthusiasm for kung fu dovetailed with the growing influence of kung fu movies—kung fu star Jet Li, for example, became a household name. The standard line among martial artists was that the kung fu we saw in the movies was only for show; it was a fundamentally different animal than the one we practiced. Stage combat was likened to *wushu*, the name the Chinese Communist Party gave to its officially sanctioned combination of Northern Shaolin, acrobatics, and dance. When Shaolin masters from the original Shaolin Temple began to open studios in big cities around the world, I was taken aback. I knew that the Shaolin Temple had been closed for more than eighty years, because I read about it, and also because Bing Gong had visited it in the early 1980s and told me that it had just reopened in the wake of the first Jet Li movie; he saw football-field-sized classes of people practicing wushu there.

It might be hard to understand how shocking this change at the end of the 1990s was to those of us who had been in the business for a while. Whenever George Xu wanted to insult somebody else's martial arts, he called it *wushu*—by which he meant "flowery and useless." When I looked in the window of these schools I saw they were using ballet barres to stretch their legs. Ballet, you know, the dance style where they wear a pink tutu! Okay, I admit, these young guys looked pretty good, (and I did three years of ballet myself) but they were also claiming to be Buddhist monks with a lineage stretching back to antiquity. It was just too much.

This trend was followed some years later by a smaller number of Daoist monks and priests from Wudang Mountain who claimed to practice "Wudang martial arts." I have to admit, they looked pretty good, too, but the story had the same problems. At an individual level, each of these teachers and performers had a lot of training and personal integrity, but were they authentic? I was under the impression that Wudang Mountain had been closed for more than a generation and that the few Daoists still practicing there had been dragged out of the mountains and through the streets by the Communist Red Guard during the Cultural Revolution (1967–1977).

On top of all this, the explosion of video on the internet made everyone an expert. Just as the *qigong* fad was waning, mixed martial arts started to gain a huge audience. Hardly anyone in the Chinese martial-arts world had any experience with ground-fighting, and almost every fight was going to the ground! Brazilian jujitsu was king.

Self-defense had long been touted as an important component of Chinese martial arts, yet, many of my martial arts friends found this dubious, there was a disconnect between what might pass for *legal* self-defense and what we were actually training. For instance, a face-to-face confrontation that one could possibly run away from was probably closer to assault, or the logic of a duel, than it was to self-defense. But heck, *it was so fun to train.*

And then I read Rory Miller's book *Meditations on Violence* (2008), and attended a workshop with him. Interacting with Rory made me feel like I was a little girl at a pajama party! Here was a former jail guard and deputy sheriff with hundreds of documented uses of force under his belt, pointing out that we martial artists had not even considered what real violence with real bad guys looks like, how they actually attack, what the act of hurting or killing does to a person emotionally, what kinds of stuff happens afterwards, and how important it is to distinguish between social and asocial violence. Violence has a logic, patterns that can be predicted; the explanations we had about the way we were training simply didn't follow that logic.

We need to reconsider what martial arts are, what they were actually invented to do, and how they developed into the arts they are today. Everyone who trains martial arts knows they are deeper than deep.

Johnstone

Finding Answers (Say "fine dancers" three times fast!)

The diversity of movement experience I cultivated early on forced me to look at things differently and to challenge the stories I was being told about martial arts along the way.

I took my first improvisational theater class from Keith Johnstone at the San Francisco Zen Center when I was fifteen. Johnstone, perhaps the foremost teacher of improvisation in the 20th Century, taught using games to dissolve fear and unlock spontaneity.[2] The experience had a huge influence on how I understand martial arts and enlightenment. In a three-day workshop, in which half the participants were Zen students, and the other half were university drama students, Johnstone put me on

---

2   Keith Johnstone's *Impro: Improvisation for the Theatre*, is required reading for my students.

the stage with this sophisticated, twenty-three year old, blonde bombshell from Stanford University. He had us sitting on a couch and set the scene: I was her visiting boyfriend, and she was babysitting and not allowed to have guests. My job was to get in her pants; her job was to get me out of the house before the parents came home. Now, that would have been enough, but in addition to that, I was given a mantra to silently repeat in my head: "I hate you, I hate you, I hate you," while her mantra was "I love you, I love you, I love you."

> ### Kung fu or Gongfu
>
> Throughout the book I use both the English word "kung fu" and the Chinese word *"gongfu."* I use "kung fu" when referring to the movies or to the subject most English speakers think of as Chinese martial arts. I use the term *"gongfu"* when referring specifically to the multiple Chinese meanings of that word. They are in fact, the same word transliterated differently.

When playing a scene like this, everything we think of as personality becomes an obstacle to acting spontaneously. What we think of as "our" personality has to be dropped in order to move the scene forward. The biggest breakthroughs I've made in martial arts are all like this, they have involved discarding something I thought of as "me."

Johnstone also had us play "status" games based on master-servant and sibling dynamics. During one of the sibling games I suddenly woke up. I realized that I was an unconscious master of the game. In my real teenage life, my sister would accuse me of something—anything, really--"Did you move my shoes?" A normal response would be, "No, why would I do that?" but a "Yes" response, followed by a clear admission of guilt—"I thought they would look better by the door,"—would trigger more accusations. If I continued to admit to whatever the accusation was (true or not) while shrinking or enlarging my physical presence, I could control her movement. It was as if we were attached by an invisible elastic force. Under normal circumstances this is a completely unconscious process, but after working with Johnstone it became conscious. I played this out with my actual sister, without telling her what I was doing; within a minute or so I had her rolling on the floor, literally tearing out her own hair. Afterwords I felt both guilty and elated at the same time. This is a bullying game. Playing it showed me that when I consciously played the victim, I was the one in control. That awakening permanently changed my relationship to criticism and authority.

Spontaneity is probably the most important skill there is for dealing with violent conflict. In conflict, posturing can be used to trigger an unconscious submissive response in an opponent, making them pliable, predictable and easy to manipulate; or, it can be used to trigger a dominance response, which is a predictably rigid attempt to communicate social dominance. In either case, experience improvising with social-status triggers creates freedom of action. It also creates the strange illusion that space can dynamically shrink and expand around people.

We are unconscious animals, driven by base urges that are deeply tied to our perception of space. Our mind evolved for movement; it is a spatial organizer, a tool that allows us to see around the rock we are climbing over, before it comes into view. Our imagination is linked to the way we move, consciously, and unconsciously. Magnetic imaging studies show that imagining an activity uses all the same parts of the brain as doing that activity, but includes the suppressive activity of the prefrontal cortex. Normally, when we use our imagination, we are suppressing movement. That's why spontaneity is often perceived as dangerous, it frees the imagination to act.

These realizations about the nature of movement, the perception of space, and the human capacity to improvise, triggered my interest in dance.

Dance-theater

When I was seventeen I got a scholarship to live in Australia for a year as an exchange student. There, I studied mime, physical theater, modern dance and composition; I had many opportunities to perform and learn stagecraft. I got into dance, partly, because it was the hardest thing I had ever tried to do. A year later, when I returned to San Francisco, I was a dancer with a seven-day-a-week discipline. San Francisco was a world center of ethnic dance, offering movement traditions from all over the world. It was a great place to get a taste of many different ways of moving; it was also a great place to go into depth. I got involved in a dynamic performing arts scene, and while continuing my studies in modern dance, improvisation, composition, and physical theater, I added ballet, North Indian, and African dance.

Malonga

Beginning in 1986, I studied Katherine Dunham Technique with her disciple, Alicia Pierce, at San Francisco State University. Dunham was a dancer, choreographer, and anthropologist who captured spectacular footage of martial dance traditions in the African diaspora during the 1930s, and collaborated with avant-garde filmmaker Maya Derren. The dance training technique she created was abstracted from the Haitian Voodoo religious context, but drew on other traditions and made creative use of a ballet barre for warmups. Pierce's classes were very demanding and very fun; they were accompanied by a group of superb drummers.

Dunham brought Malonga Casquelourd, a native of the Congo, to the United States around 1970, and he also became my teacher. He was a master dancer and drummer like nothing I had ever seen before. Malonga had an awesome physique, broad and thick like a large tree, yet fast and agile. He was able to keep complex polyrhythms going simultaneously in his voice, body, and on the drums. His father was a military officer, and as a child Malonga traveled with him all over the Congo, learning a wide array of regional dances from soldiers. Malonga was sent to mainland China in the 1960s for military training, and there he learned Mandarin. He told me an interesting story: The local Chinese government put on a dance performance for the international soldiers, made up of dances from all over the world. (The Chinese Communist art world at that point in history was engaged in a kind of international cultural absorption process.) Toward the end of the performance a group of Africans came onstage and did a dance from the Congo. Malonga was delighted, and after the show went backstage to meet his fellow countrymen. But as it turned out, they were Chinese dancers who had covered their bodies in black makeup. Malonga was in shock that they could have learned the dances and songs so well that even he didn't recognize their foreignness—put another way, they passed his unconscious authenticity test. What other training did these dancers have that made them so good?

Malonga wasn't explicitly teaching any martial arts, but he was insanely powerful, very playful, and enjoyed the occasional roughhousing interlude. I was studying martial arts simultaneously with all of this, and I started to see that everything we did in African dance had clear, highly effective fighting applications—and not just war dances; funeral dances and fishing dances had applications, too.

But even more surprising, I started to feel polyrhythms in the *liuhexinyi* I was learning from George Xu, and later in the *baguazhang* I learned from Kumar Frantzis. And I learned that my Shaolin teacher's teacher, Kuo Lien-ying, sometimes taught with a drum. I found polyrhythms were hidden in the Chinese martial arts, and knowing this was like having a key that opened up new doors. My intuition told me that many of these arts have become rhythmically flat and stale because somewhere along the line, the music got put to the side. My experience with these polyrhythms made *xinyiquan and baguazhang* easier to learn.

It is amazing how much martial arts can be found in popular dance styles if one has experience with the elements of fighting. Even a dance like the waltz can improve a student's ability to manipulate momentum in a spin.

The concept of *swing* in the American dance tradition, called *ginga* in Brazilian samba and capoeira dance, essentially means the ability to fight.[3] Well, not exactly; *swing* means a hidden feeling, a rhythmic feeling of potential power, not obvious, but essential. In other words, swing can refer to sexiness, too; it isn't *applied* power or technique, but rather potential power. It is space in the rhythm, and in one's body, to play. The martial origins and martial prowess of these dances have been obscured in the twentieth century so that now there are great numbers of people thinking they are doing swing, who are in fact just doing the outer forms. Truly, *it don't mean a thing if it ain't got that swing.* Something similar seemed to have happened to Chinese martial arts.

Chitresh Das

At the same time I was studying African dance, I also started studying *kathak*, a form of North Indian classical dance, with Chitresh Das. Das was a consummate improviser. In our first class he channeled the harsh nuns he had known attending Catholic Schools in India, Rambo with a machine gun, and pop star Michael Jackson—all within the strict rhythmic structures of Indian classical music. No one else in India did *kathak* like Chitresh Das, but if you've never seen it, it is a form of storytelling, sort of like tap-dance and flamenco done barefoot with five pounds of bells wrapped around each ankle. Das explained that *kathak* was developed by Rajput warriors and then moved into the Mughal courts of Lucknow. As the Mughals fell from power, many dancers fell into the role of courtesans. Again, martial arts were not taught explicitly, although Chitresh Das had boxed in his youth, and if you've ever tried dueling with blades you know that rhythmic footwork with speed and power is a handy thing to have. *Kathak* also incorporates body technique that can be used as chops, sweeps, and elbow strikes; movements that

---

3   Cristina F. Rosa, *Brazilian Bodies and Their Choreographies of Identification: Swing Nation.* Palgrave Macmillan, 2015.

can be used to apply joint locks; and drop steps, lots of drop steps. These martial elements in *kathak* are called *tandava*. (I have since learned that there are other theatrical martial dances in India that are more explicit about their fighting prowess and purpose, like *chhau*, *kalarippayattu*, and *thang ta*.)

The bronze bells worn for *kathak* are strung tightly together with open facets. From a martial point of view, they served as armor for the ankles designed to catch blades, and as weights for developing power; historically, a force of thousands of men wearing them on the battlefield all stamping their feet was intended to terrify the enemy. This is described in the ancient epic, the *Mahabharata*.

Kathak also shares many of the hand techniques and arm movement patterns used in the southern styles of Chinese martial arts.

These experiences provoked a lot of questions. My martial-arts teachers Bing Gong and George Xu were great performers, although they didn't aspire to be; they incorporated many complex elements of performing skill, specific technologies of the stage I could point to and name. Could that have been an accident? Or was theater training secretly infused in the martial arts? And if so, why? And perhaps even more importantly, if I was learning a performing art along with these fighting skills, why didn't my teachers know that? Why didn't their stories about the origins of the art match the art as it actually was?

Oomoto

What is ritual; and what is ritual theater?

When I was twenty I attended a three-month summer program in Japan at a Shinto religious organization called Oomoto. Oomoto got its start in the early twentieth century as a cult centered around a woman who did spirit writing. This illiterate woman named Nao had a bit of a Cinderella story: she walked outside one winter morning and poured a large bucket of ice water on her head, and then evidently went into some sort of trance. After this event she began writing, eventually producing some 20,000 poems. She would see letters in golden light on a blank page and would simply fill them in with black ink. The poems quickly revealed that she was possessed by a dragon prince who foresaw the end-times and a great rebirth of humanity as a unified whole.

The Oomoto organization grew under the influence of Onisaburo Deguchi, Nao's husband. In the lead-up to World War II, the organization was in conflict with the imperial government, and Onisaburo ended up in prison in Manchuria, along with his friend, the future founder of Aikido, Morihei Ueshiba, who is probably Oomoto's most famous member.

I ended up at Oomoto because my father had decided that college wasn't important. To assuage his lingering guilt about not paying for our education, he sent his three children to learn traditional Japanese arts instead. Broadly speaking, the Shinto religion—which, with Buddhism, is prevalent in Japan—worships nature and natural phenomena. Because traditional Japanese art is often an exploration or a representation of nature, artists are held in very high esteem, almost as ambassadors of the gods. Thus, Oomoto had a summer "missionary" program in which the students from both inside and outside Japan learned four traditional arts: *budo* (martial ways), *shodo* (calligraphy), *shimai* (dance interludes for Noh drama), and *chado* (tea ceremony). Each of the arts was taught in a ritual context, and had specific implements and attachments that we carried to the dance hall, the tea house, or the dojo; for each art we wore traditional clothing, each with its own specific way of tying knots.

The calligraphy class began with each of us sitting in meditation in the *seiza* (kneeling) position. Our teacher had really long eyebrows, and when he came in, he would sit down and begin singing. Except he wasn't singing words, he was singing some kind of wild improvised animal sounds; deep, guttural, and formless. This would last about twenty minutes, and then for about ten minutes we would make ink on our own individual ink stones by rubbing an ink stick in a small pool of water. After that we would work on writing a single character. I think it is possible that my calligraphy improved over the three months, although I'm left-handed and was required to use my right hand, so I think it probably did something strange to my brain as well. In any event, it was impossible to find the lines between religion, art, and a really strange teacher. This realm, where charisma, spontaneity, and routine practice meet, is characteristic of ritual.

I was self-identifying as a dancer at the time, but strangely enough, the *shimai* (dance interludes) we learned felt confining to me. *Shimai*, at a few minutes each, are much shorter than the six-to-twelve-hour-long Noh plays. The movement of *shimai* is generally faster than the movement of Noh drama, but not faster than the average *taijiquan* form. The content was tragic—people dying, loss, unfulfilled love, that kind of thing. The challenge for me was to move less. Although *shimai* dancers do not wear masks, the facial expressions are mask-like, unchanging, so all emotion and story must be told with the subtle movements of the body, self-accompanied by a single-sentence song. It was explained to us that our bodies should be as empty as possible. When one student asked what we should be thinking while performing, the teacher answered simply, "This foot goes here." The stage where we practiced was a box with a roof which had a bridge leading to it from stage right, for long slow entrances. At the back of the stage was a tree on the wall. It was explained to us that the tree was the conduit for spirits to enter our bodies. When one of us asked if we should expect this to happen, our teacher explained that if we were completely empty, it might, but that this generally only happened to seasoned performers; however, we should watch attentively, because it was sometimes difficult to tell. Did they mean that emptiness brought the spirit in and precise form kept it under control? Or that the precise representation of the story and character invited the spirit in and the emptiness contained it? Although I had no comprehension of it at the time, the spirits we were representing were originally vengeful ghosts; this type of dance is a ritual for transforming them into helpful spirits.

We were somewhat taken aback by the instructions we got on a field trip we took to a six-hour-long professional Noh performance, "It's okay to fall asleep during the performance; you may expect to hear some people snoring."

The performance that day, over twenty-five years ago, is seared in my brain. Naturally, given permission, I did fall asleep. I couldn't help it—it was *so* slow. A single character could easily spend half an hour just crossing the bridge to get to the stage. The music and costumes were spectacular for ten, even fifteen minutes, but then I got this overwhelming feeling that *nothing* was happening. Sleep overtook me. Then, opening my eyes for a moment, I saw a black and gold demon with crazy red hair entering the stage. I fought wildly to keep my eyes open, but I blinked and he was on the other side of the bridge; I blinked again and he was coming down stage toward me stamping and snorting, and then suddenly he was right above me, dancing. *Wake up!* I told myself, but I couldn't; the demon had entered my dreams.

The experience was one in which theater and ritual were merged. Narrative, music, spectacle, and altered states of consciousness were incorporated into the performance context—for both the performers and the audience.

Budo class was held in a handmade wooden building. The dojo floor was covered by handmade *tatami* mats, surrounded on three sides by handmade *shoji* paper screen doors. We would begin sitting in *seiza*—bowing, of course, on the way into the room. We were a group of less than ten students, and there were almost as many assistant teachers. The head teacher would open the *shoji* screen in the middle of the north wall to reveal a simple garden with a spectacular plum tree perfectly framed. (The plum tree is a symbol of rebirth at the end of winter.) We would then all chant a chant about Oomoto. I asked several native Japanese speakers what the words we were chanting meant, but they told me it was archaic and indecipherable except for the repetition of the word *protection*. For *budo* we used a single-edged, two-handed, straight, wooden sword. We practiced a handful of stepping and striking movements solo, but most of the class was dedicated to two-person practice. We did sword-against-sword training, and disarms with or without a sword. We performed for an audience at the end of the summer. The best things, speaking in retrospect as a martial artist, were the simple, direct efficiency of the movement and the use of spontaneous timing even when we knew exactly what was going to happen. Playing with that element of time is incredibly useful in martial arts training.

Again, this practice contained numerous elements of ritual: exquisite *fengshui*; simple, clear, utilitarian, and profoundly moving surroundings; repetitive, efficient action mixed with spontaneity; and the invocation of some unseen force, *protection*.

I don't consider my *budo* training to be a martial art in the Chinese sense. It didn't have a form—a *taolu*—and it was much more simple and direct than any other martial art I've studied. There was no claim that it was an art of self-defense. It wasn't connected to anything on a battlefield; we practiced barefoot. In Japan, the martial arts, like so much of the culture, are highly ritualized. Ritualization is tied to one's sense of personhood; ritualization in Japan takes the place of character development in the West. The way we moved in *budo* was very much like modern Aikido, which is universally considered a martial art. And like Aikido, it was embedded in Shinto ritual. I think, as a point of comparison, Chinese martial arts has very little ritualization, the movement itself *is* the ritual—a point we will return to later in the book.

And finally we practiced tea ceremony. This was by far my favorite art, and one I would later return to as a daily practice.

Tea ceremony is very, very simple. A guest enters a simple hut, looks around, and sits down. The host offers a bean-paste sweet and then a bowl of tea. The guest drinks the tea. The guest looks around and leaves. That's it.

There is a solo form, in which the *"guest"* is all sentient beings for all time. There are group versions. There are sometimes meals outside the tea house beforehand, or thin teas served after midnight. There are many variations and three major schools.

Tea ceremony was created for samurai warriors at a time when they were killing each other at the drop of a hat. The first requirement of tea ceremony was that the sword be left outside the tea hut. There are many different types of tea huts; they are all unique, but the way one enters, walks, looks at the calligraphy, looks at the flower arrangement, or holds a napkin—this movement is all precisely prescribed. The quality of one's steps, how many, how big they are, which foot goes first—it is all precisely prescribed. The same goes for what is said: "Please enjoy the sweet," "Thank you, I will now eat the sweet." "Please have some tea," "I will now drink the tea." For samurai warriors on the edge of their seats, one false move would have had everyone reaching for an improvised weapon.

It is a very *potent* space to be in. The smallest change in the quality of a gesture gets noticed. There is a feeling that every tiny movement is embedded with meaning. When normal action and interaction is so contained, all the senses—and especially the imagination—run wild. *This is a major characteristic of ritual.*

The flowers in the arrangement must be picked wild, and if the ceremony takes place at night, they must be white. The implements follow the esthetic principle of *wabi-sabi*; that is, some are funky, old, chunky and rough, while others are exquisite, stylized, glimmering and smooth. They create a feeling of harmony and unbounded inclusion, as if part of the purpose of the ritual is to soften preferences.

Tea ceremony is a feast for the senses. As a guest I would have been overflowing with appreciation, only there is no place for that in the ritual. It is as if the only option is to turn that appreciation inward and contain it. And what good would it do, anyway, to point out one moment of beauty to the exclusion of all the rest? It would seem false.

Certain elements of spontaneity are ritually embedded in the tea ceremony. For instance, the lead guest may ask a short, simple question about the appearance of the tea bowl or the provenance of the tea scoop. The host may answer. There are other elements of spontaneity, to be sure, and this is very difficult to describe, but I suppose these must be found in the feeling of infinite space and time that is the essence of ritual.

One day they had us come an hour and a half early to tea class so that we could see how the tea hut was prepared and help clean. I was given a scrub brush and a white five-gallon bucket with clear water in it. They sat me in the garden in front of a pile of smooth, clean river rocks and told me to scrub the rocks. I guess there were about three hundred pounds of fist-sized rocks. I gamely picked up a rock and started scrubbing; I wasn't sure when to stop, because the rocks weren't dirty, but after a few seconds I put the wet rock down and picked up another one. After about five minutes the first rocks I had "cleaned" were dry, and I realized that I had no idea which rocks I had already cleaned. Did I need a method for this madness? Did it matter if I just scrubbed one rock for the entire hour and a half? We all had strange jobs; I think one student's job was to pick up all the leaves that were on rocks and then put some of them back down in a random way. I cannot claim to understand it, but simply put, this experience opened my eyes. It caused me to *look* at things. I would describe the shift as physiological rather than mental.

One of the tea implements that everyone carries is a fine silk handkerchief, which is used for wiping other implements. It gets folded and re-folded repeatedly in very precise ways. One day our tea teacher was making tea for us, and I noticed a disturbance in the room—a kind of excitement, I guess, since we weren't supposed to be moving or saying anything. Then I noticed it: our tea teacher was using a Snoopy handkerchief for the ritual, though his face gave away nothing. And then it started, the urge to laugh. I practically had to rearrange all my internal organs to contain it.

I've taken this detour into my experiences in Japan because they were so useful for me in trying to understand what Chinese ritual culture was like before the twentieth century. It is not to say that one type of ritual is necessarily like another; rather, that attempting to understand ritual by any method other than direct experience is absurd.

Daoism

After traveling to India in 1994, I became disillusioned with Indian dance. Not with the actual dance per se, or my teacher, but with the horrors of the caste system and the way dance fit into it. I felt betrayed. How could I have put six years of intellectual and somatic effort into embodying this art only to realize, once I was in India, that I had been overlaying my culture's values on top of a tradition with altogether different values and meaning? I also realized that what was most exciting to me about *kathak* was the ability of my teacher, Chitresh Das, to improvise. What I found in India was that the tradition of improvisation had atrophied; in its place I found the perpetuation of hierarchies and birth lineages at the expense of merit[4]

That experience led me to question martial arts as well. Lineages have value because they pass on knowledge in depth, but without spontaneity and renewal they can become ghostly practices, dislodged from meaning and values. I wanted insider knowledge and experience of Chinese culture. I wanted to figure out how to recreate the vibrant milieu that originally spawned the martial arts in China. It was this desire that led me to study Daoism with Liu Ming.

Daoism is essentially a practice-based religious tradition built around the idea that renewal is continuously available. Daoism has always been centered around lineages, with experimentalists out on the edges. Those experimentalists have continuously inspired changes, while the lineages have created continuity.

The central practice of Daoism is ritual. These rituals contain meditation and movement traditions, while also being storehouses of knowledge and narrative. Urban, rural, and national versions of Daoist ritual have always had a relationship to hermits and hermit culture. Hermits retreat, and live apart, in an asocial setting. The hermit culture, which offers the opportunity to leave society and then return, has functioned within Daoism as a great source of both spontaneous renewal and experimental depth.

Daoism has been in continuous development for a couple thousand years, has a vast canon of texts, and enormous local diversity. All of it is centered around the *Daodejing*, a sacred text in eighty-one chapters, attributed to Laozi. Over the nine years I studied with Liu Ming, he had me recite a chapter of the *Daodejing* for at least fifteen minutes every day; I also had to read traditional commentaries on that chapter. The main subject of the *Daodejing* is a concept that has been summarized by the term *wuwei*—variously translated as not-doing, non-aggression, without pretense, or non-conceptual awareness.

The Daoist training I received was practice-oriented, but it wasn't method-oriented. What I mean by that is, we were discouraged from seeing any particular method as the source of changes in our perception; rather, we would investigate what the original "view" was that suggested

---

4   From 1994 until his death in 2014, Chitresh Das worked diligently to bring improvisational dance back to India, where it had become a rarity.

a given "method," and then consider how practicing that method changed the original view. For example, Liu Ming had us practicing a solo form of Japanese tea ceremony before doing an hour or more of meditation each morning. He encouraged us to construct an ideal space called a "quiet room" for these two practices. I turned a walk-in closet with a small window into an elevated and dedicated space for practice; it had *shoji* screens (sliding paper doors), *tatami* mats, and faux gold-leaf walls. One of the basic "methods" of tea ceremony is to handle heavy implements as if they are light, and to treat lightweight implements as if they are heavy. Now what was the purpose of this "method"? What was the original "view" which suggested making tea that way? And then, once we had been doing it for a while, what was the effect? How did the "fruition" of that practice change how we saw its original intended purpose?

Perhaps the original idea was that treating heavy objects as if they were light would cause me to pay extra attention to what I was doing. If this was true, then once I was expert at picking up objects and putting them down, I could drop the "method." On the other hand, perhaps the original idea was to demonstrate the illusory nature of perception. In which case, I should have been getting better and better at creating a sort of magic trick for the eyes. But strangely, the effect of this "method" was that picking up a light tea bowl as if it were a heavy one caused me to change my entire body. In fact, doing it every day changed the way I thought about what a person is. It is hard to construct an argument that the method itself does that. How could such a simple method cause me to notice that the way my body felt was determined by how I perceived and handled the objects around me? Was I an active free agent in this process? A method is actually inseparable from the vision (or orientation) from which we practice it. But the fruition of practicing a given method can change our perceptions of the world around us, and thus, if we let it, change our view of the purpose and meaning of that method.

Liu Ming lived in a home in Santa Cruz we called the *tan*, which means "altar," but also carries the meaning of the community that supports the altar. Several community members made a living doing construction of various sorts, and since I was good with tools and willing to help, I was usually part of *tan* construction projects. The first thing I remember was moving the front door to a new location. The project involved cutting out, and then sealing up, walls; building stairs; painting; and other finish work. After about a month, we moved the front door again. Then, about a year later, we moved it again. The same thing happened with two of the ceilings we installed with complex decorative structures: after we finished, we then reinstalled them with different designs, first higher, then lower. We altered various pathways from room to room, built a couple of experimental tea rooms and a library, fitted and refitted fixtures. The landscape, too, was constantly changing: we packed earth for a small mountain and grew a bamboo forest, only to move them around later. At first, this was shocking: "We just did that! —Really? We're going to move it again?" But the process was fun. I couldn't tell if Liu Ming was being incredibly fickle or if something else was going on. He used these opportunities to teach us about *fengshui* and its connection to ritual exorcism. These were experiments with everyday spatial perception, the subtleties of coming in and out of rooms and moving around spaces. He seemed to be teaching something about impermanence, about the ability to drop preferences. Perhaps conditioning the habit of taking a second look at the things we take for granted—what is it about a given thing that makes it important? Or maybe he was just fickle. I'm not sure there is a difference. These sorts of conversations were further developed in our text study groups.

All of this had a profound effect on the way I practiced martial arts.

I went into hermit retreat mode for about five years. Besides the "quiet room" in my apartment, I got rid of all my furniture so I had a space to dance, and I practiced saying no to social activities and obligations. I was teaching martial arts, but I cut my hours to a minimum. I closely adhered to the auspices of the Daoist calendar (*Tongshu*). Occasionally a request came on a particularly auspicious day for social activity and I would say yes. The Daoist calendar allowed me to externalize my decision making. I tossed aside my personal preferences. The counterintuitive result was that I had lots of free time to do whatever I wanted. The people we have around us, and the patterns we establish, define us. Putting aside my personal preferences for a few years, without actually going anywhere, gave me a type of freedom I didn't know I had.

This book isn't specifically about Daoism, but Daoism is a part of me, and it deeply informs my perspective on Chinese culture and martial arts.

George Xu and Teaching Emptiness

I started teaching martial arts, gymnastics, and dance to kids when I was in my twenties. From the beginning, theatrical improvisation and offering opportunities to perform were part of my teaching style.

Over the years I developed a program in public schools under the title "World Dance," which allowed me to combine my skills. As I developed experience I focused on teaching martial arts, adding drums, gongs, and wood blocks, and incorporating these other skills. This was a novel approach when I started doing it, but now that I know the history of the arts better, I see that I was simply reinventing tradition.

In my twenties I also started teaching adults. The amazing people who have come to study with me over the years have also been my teachers, and teaching has made me a better person. Like many teachers who love the depth of these arts, I have often wished that my students would set out to learn the whole art. This is one of the reasons I'm writing this book. In talking to other martial arts teachers, I find they often have a similar wish. The subject—the years of study, the depth of investigation and experimentation—is deeper and more complex than anyone can see at the outset. Even students who have studied for years often fail to see the depth of the arts. This inability to see, often followed by disillusionment, is a big reason people quit. The remedy, I think, is to offer a much broader view of what the arts are—a framework, a 360-degree view—that will allow students to see the depth their teachers have to offer and also aid teachers in revealing that depth. Getting the story right, matching the origins of martial arts to the actual arts as they are practiced, is a good place to start.

Lastly, I'd like to further acknowledge George Xu. After fifteen years away from him, studying with other teachers and becoming immersed in Daoism, I returned to find that he had completely reformed and redesigned the way he practiced martial arts. His inspiration has continued to have a profound effect on me. George Xu discovered, via a sort of reverse engineering, some of the core practices of Daoism inside internal martial arts. He had replaced toughness with emptiness, and put it at the center of training. This newly inspired practice allowed me to make stronger connections between the theatrical and religious traditions I was steeped in.

Why write a book about the possible origins of Chinese martial arts, rather than the probable origins? Because I'm less interested in hard conclusions than I am in being open to the possibilities.

Understanding all the ingredients that went into the soup called martial arts is a process of looking at how, over the years, martial arts have interacted with diverse elements of society. By having a better understanding what martial arts were, we can better understand what they are.

A reader at this point would be forgiven for thinking, hey, I do martial arts—I know what they are! I know them because I do them. But that actually gets to the heart of the problem. The martial arts I have practiced for thirty-five years and counting are made up of lots of stuff that isn't all that easy to explain. As much as I'm passionate about the arts, I still find aspects of them perplexing, and I find it difficult to explain why someone in the past would invent things the way they did. We all have blind spots—limitations we don't know we have. I want to discover the blind spots of the people who created martial arts, and I want to expose my own blind spots too!

The simple truth is that the origins of Chinese martial arts were already obscure at the beginning of the twentieth century, and were then further obscured by various political movements. They have outlived memory. Even if we could talk to someone from, say, 1550, or 1830, their way of life would be so different from ours that it might be impossible to understand them. But it is just this difficulty that makes the quest interesting. What are the possible origins?

Three Perspectives

The following three chapters offer three different views of the notion that martial arts, theater, and religion are a single subject. The first chapter explores elements of religion and theater embedded in the martial arts. This chapter is the most immediately accessible because it is written from the perspective of someone practicing martial arts and discovering theatricality and religiosity in the practice.

The second chapter looks at martial arts and religion embedded in theater. Here, evidence about the characteristics, history, and function of theatrical traditions in China will show that theater is inseparable from martial arts and religion.

The third, forth, and fifth chapters look at how Chinese religions incorporate martial arts and theater. These are the most difficult chapters to grasp because Chinese religion defies simple categorizations. Religion in China was an embodied tradition—scholars sometimes use the term orthopraxy, rather than orthodoxy, because belief was never at the center of Chinese religious expression—it has always been action-oriented. Looking at specific realms in which religion incorporated theatricality and martial movement will reframe martial arts as a key element of Chinese religions.

The sixth chapter shifts gears, explaining the recent historical process by which theater, martial arts and religion came to be seen as distinct subjects. This misperception has many elements, which all converge in a world-view that does not match the facts.

Chapter seventh is a chance to reflect on the significance of all this. What does it mean? Why does it matter? What is inspiring about it? Where do we go from here?

Martial Skills

Modeling Righteousness

The most common reason people give for putting their children in martial arts classes is so that they will learn how to act with moral self-discipline. The list of qualities that the average parent wants their kid to learn in martial arts classes includes leadership, protecting the weak, legal and moral self-defense, overcoming challenges, persistence in the face of adversity, seeing the big picture, self-discipline, self-improvement, self-motivation, cooperation, teamwork, body confidence and awareness, love of exercise, learning from failures, and the ability to concentrate and focus. That is a lot of expectations to have! Why, if the main purpose of martial arts was fighting, would this ever have come about? The answer is simple: martial arts were always about more than fighting.

For most of the last thousand years, the vast majority of people in China got their models of righteousness from theatrical characters on the stage. Many of the heroes, villains, judges, and comics of the stage were based on actual historic figures like the honest, brave and righteous General Guan Gong, a hero who lived in the second century and was immortalized in a collection of plays called *The Three Kingdoms*. Guan Gong, like many of the characters of Chinese theater was made into a god—in this case, the god of war and accounting. (He is the god of accounting because he was jailed at one point, and during his incarceration the guards fed him, secretly he kept track of exactly how much food he was given and upon his release he surprised the guards by paying them the exact value of the food he had been given. That precision and honesty is one of the reasons a small statue of Guan Gong with his halberd, big belly, enlarged liver and red face is seen facing the door in the back of so many Chinese businesses around the world.)

What we call martial arts training today was the basic training for playing character roles like Guan Gong on the stage. The large generals and judge characters of the Chinese stage, like Guan Gong, all used similar physical theater training; they walked around in horse stance, giving orders and fighting. The horse stance used in martial-arts classes everywhere is the same as the horse stance used in theater. While there is a great deal that goes into training a traditional professional actor, the base movements are identical to those used in martial-arts classes.

There are, of course, many, many other character roles in Chinese theater traditions. Sun Wukong, the monkey king, is a huge favorite of parents and children alike. In the epic story *Journey to the West*, the comic monkey king starts out good-natured but wild, a chaotic force that needs to be contained. As he becomes more powerful he also becomes a better person…er…monkey, and eventually reaches enlightenment. His given name, "*Wukong*," is a joke that shifts in meaning throughout the story as he attains emptiness; it can mean "so vacuous," "aware of vacuity," "not empty," "unable to empty," and eventually means "supremely empty." In his character role on the stage and as a popular god installed in countless temples, Sun Wukong represents a kind of contained wildness that can be used in the service of righteousness.

The idea of contained wildness can be found in nearly every Chinese martial-arts class: students bow with their right hand made into a fist and covered by their left hand. I have heard many different explanations for the symbolism of this action, some of them cosmological, like the sun and the moon, or yin and yang; but the explanation I offer students is that when you put your hand into a fist you are committing to develop maximum explosive power, and when you put your open hand on top of it, you are committing to develop the ability to control it—just like Sun Wukong and the other great hero-gods of the Chinese theater.

The physicality of learning martial arts was closely associated with character roles. Once upon a time, when students learned the movements they were acting out the righteousness and playfulness of characters from the countless Chinese theatrical narratives about martial prowess. They were practicing taking on the physicality and manners of great leaders they knew from the stage, like Guan Gong, or the qualities of a great and loyal friend, like the bandit-hero Wu Song from *Outlaws of the Marsh*.

Through the daily rigors of training, students of martial arts demonstrate the discipline, motivation, and self-improvement of Mulian, who traveled to Hell and back to save his mother. (Before the

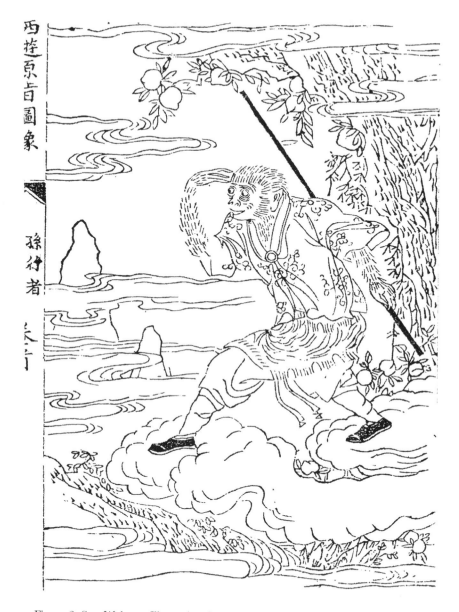

西遊原旨圖象

孫行者

Figure 2. Sun Wukong, Illustration from the *Original Gist of the Journey to the West (Xiyou Yuanzhĭ Tuxiang)*, 19th Century. Courtesy of Wikimedia Commons.

twentieth century, *Mulian Rescues His Mother* was an important ritual play, widely performed as part of the liturgical calendar of Southern China. Much like Americans see *Snow White* and *Cinderella*, to grow up in China and not be familiar with such common plays and their heroes would have been nearly impossible.)

Mind Training

Ask students to quiet their tongues and empty their minds of words. Encourage them to use their bodies to sense the world around them, to broaden their awareness of everything going on, to take in as much information and sensation as possible. Stimulate their senses, push range of motion, make demands beyond what they think is too difficult—from extraordinary balance to maximum explosive power. Put students into chaotic situations and then suddenly demand order. Force them out of themselves—be violent, intense, creative, sensitive, nurturing, cooperative, freeing; and for heaven's sake, push the limits of fun—and for some reason, afterwards, their ability to focus will be second nature.

Doing martial arts trains the mind. While hardly anyone would argue with that statement, it is often assumed that the specific mind-training elements of martial arts are peripheral or have been tacked on as an afterthought. Mind training is often considered religious; yet many martial-arts teachers encourage students to take up seated meditation because it will help make them better martial artists—physically, emotionally, and morally. Martial arts without mind training would be hollow and incomplete.

This is not an instructional book. Martial artists may want to reclaim, or discard, the following types of mind training, and that is fine; but my purpose is to show that they are all organically connected to martial arts.

The five categories of mind training I have identified are: 1) stillness 2) visualization, 3) trance-mediumship, 4) shamanic allies, and 5) the various types of awareness which are also common in the West, like emotional maturity and operant conditioning. I will examine them one by one.

Stillness

Chan Buddhist meditation (called Zen in Japan) is a non-conceptual practice. One sits in the correct upright posture; that's it. There may be esoteric instructions—not-knowing, non-aggression, being without preference—but the method is profoundly simple. The same method is called Zuowang (sitting and forgetting) in Daoism; in Tibetan Buddhism the non-conceptual approach is called Dzogchen (Great Perfection).

The same practice can be done standing up; just maintain stillness, that's the whole teaching. Any specific sort of focus—intent, chanting, mantras, visualizations, or other goals—belongs to other methods; they are different practices. With this type of meditation, there is no distinction between the method itself and the fruition of the method; they are one and the same. The easiest way to establish this experience is to construct an environment for practicing without distractions. In China this was called a Quiet Room, and was a space dedicated exclusively to this practice, usually with an open wall or window looking out to a simple garden or natural setting. This room became the model for the dojo in Japan, an ideal place to practice. A walled garden is also a perfect environment for the practice of standing meditation. In China, temples were a traditional place to practice martial arts—they contained walled courtyards for meritorious community events—which otherwise remained empty.

This singular non-conceptual method permeates the practice of martial arts, and has always given teachers permission to say, "Don't ask questions, just practice." (Or in the words of Yoda, "There is no try— only do.") The establishment of the experience of emptiness is the most fundamental element of martial arts practice. Sometimes this emptiness is described as constancy: limitless devotion or discipline. As easy as emptiness is to establish, it is also easy to stray from. Devotion which has an object of focus is not emptiness; nor are nameable accomplishments like belts, awards, or rank.

Visualization

Buddhism, Daoism, and Dzogchen all have esoteric visualization practices. The practice I am most familiar with from Daoism is called *jindan*, the golden elixir.[5] The non-conceptual practice of Zuowang is

---

5   *Jindan,* the *"golden elixir,"* is part of a larger category of Daoist practices called *neidan* which means "inner elixir." The word "dan" is common to both terms and literally means cinnabar. Cinnabar is a natural substance that when heated releases mercury, the only metal that is liquid at room temperature. In ancient alchemy there was great enthusiasm for heating cinnabar in furnaces under special conditions with rare ingredients to produce magical elixirs. This category of meditation practices uses terms from ancient alchemy as metaphors for transformation.

the ground on which *jindan* is practiced. The experience of emptiness becomes like a stage, or a platform, on which *jindan* takes place. *Jindan* is an open-ended tradition with hundreds of documented variants; however, the core of the practice is unvarying. It has three components: *jing*, substance; *qi*, animation; and *shen*, imagination. The central teaching of *jindan* is this: In stillness, *jing* and *qi* distill, they become distinct; from there, an active spatial imagination *(shen)* can transform limitations. If someone slaps me on the face while I remain still, I will feel my face (jing), but I will also feel heat and vibration rising off of it *(qi)*. That is called the distillation of *jing* and *qi*. Whether the slap hurts, or causes me to burst out laughing, depends entirely on what I imagine *(shen)* the purpose and meaning of the slap to be. The practice of *jindan* is based on an experience of being—which is always true, and always operative.

Jindan is the establishment of an order of action, whereby the spatial imagination leads the physical body, with *qi* as an intermediary between the two. This concept is the foundation of all forms of Daoist ritual. As a concept, it is the subject of countless works of art, including poetry, plays, ceramics, and, of course, martial arts.

Jindan is at the center of traditional Chinese concepts about death. The idea that a person can perfect their body at or before the moment of death, and thus free their imagination to join with the Dao, is called *xian*; it is usually translated as "immortal" in English. The practice of *jindan* is a key element of funerals (and other rituals), where it is used for resolving the lingering influences of the dead.

I will return to the topic of *jindan* in future chapters. But before leaving it, for the sake of intellectual integrity, I would like to take a detour and respond to some popular ideas about what *jindan* is. This is important because the same ideas affect the way martial arts are misperceived. I chose the provocative image of being slapped in the face as a description of *jindan* in order to counter the general practice of couching it in difficult-to-access metaphysical language. Mystical Christianity and its New-Age descendants impose this language on Daoism by framing *jindan* in terms of beliefs. If I get slapped and I see a purple mist raising up around my cheek, that is my imagination *(shen)*. Imagination is a real thing, not a metaphysical concept. And whether or not I believe the mist is real, is an irrelevant insinuation. What matters, for *jindan* is whether I *experience* the mist as real—whether I see it and feel it. Imagination has real impact in the real world; without it, problems would not get solved. *Jindan* is the perfection of the body as a vehicle for expressing the imagination. Could we say the same thing about the martial arts?

Trance-mediumship

Trance-mediumship was a central part of Chinese religion. The idea that spirits—ghosts, demons, gods, and immortals—could possess a person's body was ubiquitous. For instance, it was part of the criminal-justice system: long ago if a person had been murdered without witnesses, a trance-medium could be brought into court to channel the dead person. The medium would then ask the dead person directly, "Who killed you?"

In Taiwan today, there are women who are experts at channeling the dead. There is also a type of ritual expert called a *tangki*, who has a personal relationship with a specific god, and performs public rituals as that god—Sun Wukong, the Monkey King, for instance; or Guan Gong, the god of war.

The Chinese scholarly tradition over the last five hundred years often used trance-medium methods to channel both poetry and sacred texts directly from immortals like Lu Dongbin, the head of the Eight Immortals, or Zhang Sanfeng, a noted practitioner of *jindan* and the purported creator of *taijiquan*. A significant portion of the Daoist canon was created this way.

While it is poorly documented, illiterate practitioners of the martial arts likely used these same methods to create some of the forms *(taolu)* that are practiced today. A medium would go into trance, become a god, and teach a martial-arts form.

A characteristic of trance-mediums in Chinese culture is that they have no memory of what happened while they were possessed. This type of trance was used extensively in warfare over hundreds of years. The best known example of this, because it was covered extensively by European, Japanese, and American newspapers, was the Boxer Rebellion (1898–1900), in which Chinese combatants believed they were bulletproof while possessed by various gods of the theater.

Shamanism

Shamanism is less important to Chinese religion than other forms of training the mind, but it has a place in the development of warfare and religion, and thus influenced the development of martial arts.

Shamans go on dangerous mystical journeys; often using drugs, or dancing to the point of exhaustion. In this altered state they court an ally, such as a snake spirit, a river demon, or a tiger god. When the shaman recovers, she can then call on that spirit-ally to aid in battle or healing—thus granting her the symbolic powers of a snake, a river, or a tiger. The lingering shamanic roots of martial arts are evident in many animals forms and styles, particularly in the way practitioners utilize the qualities of animals, like the snake and the crane, to express power.

The first four types of mind training stillness, visualization, trance-mediumship, and shamanic allies are usually considered part of religion in the West and modern China alike, but historically they were not separate from martial arts or theater. The fifth type of mind training is claimed by modernity as a purely secular development, but it was originally integrated with religion, theater, and martial arts.

Awareness

Many ways of training the mind that were part of traditional martial-arts training are also popular in Euro-America. The ability to focus, concentrate, and persevere in the face of adversity are so integral to the martial arts—and education in general—that they hardly need mentioning. The same is true for emotional maturity, personal responsibility, and compassion.

Some mind training instills automatic reactions. This is called operant conditioning, and there are many uses for it. For instance, many martial-arts schools today will teach scenarios in which the student practices pushing the "go button." Scenario training is a way to rehearse problem-solving through imagining and acting out situations where a violent response may be appropriate. Operant conditioning presents high-intensity situations in which a particular movement, or type of movement, may need to be executed suddenly and explosively—it is a way to prepare for acts of moral integrity which demand decisive action.

This type of training often triggers intense soul-searching and conflicting emotions in students, because violence is formative—it has the potential to re-form identity. In its simplest form, martial-arts training builds moral character. But taken beyond the ordinary, experiences with violence can reveal that the self is an illusion, which allows one to transcend the limitations of identity. This core concept of many enlightenment traditions is integrated into the very foundation of martial arts training.

Rory Miller suggests, in *Meditations on Violence*, that we have the story of enlightenment backwards. Retreating to the mountains doesn't cause enlightenment. Those secluded hermits of yore were trying to replicate the mind-states of former warriors whom they had met because they were also hiding in the mountains. Hermits encountered rare individuals whose identity and sense of self had been utterly transformed in battle—*before* their retreat into the mountains.

The Elixir of Ceramics

The practice of jindan has been expressed with artistic metaphor countless times; we might even say it is the central metaphor of Chinese classical art. A good example comes from the field of ceramics. To throw a vessel on a pottery wheel requires the potter to be very still and to move with continuous flowing actions. A vessel is empty on the inside, instilled with the potter's vitality *(qi)* and stillness. Once the vessel is complete, it is glazed and fired in a kiln. Chinese glazes were developed spontaneously from airborne wood ash adhering to the pots within enormous dragon kilns built into the sides of mountains. Over time, glazes were developed by combining wood ash with a composite of elements called feldspar. As the heat in the kiln increases, the glaze bubbles and foams out several inches off of the pot making it appear to double in size. As the temperature of the kiln rises further, the glaze turns to smooth glass and chemically bonds to the vessel. At this point the kiln will be cooled slowly. Chinese potters discovered that, by controlling the amount of air in the kiln as it cooled, they could create a pressurized environment (now called a reduction, because the amount of oxygen in the kiln has been reduced, forcing oxygen-bonding molecules to the surface of the vessel). Depending on how intense the reduction is and the constituents of the glaze, the colors that result go from a soft sky-blue to a deep red. And there is a perfect quantum reduction in between light blue and red where purples will appear. Pottery made red is called Ox Blood; light blues and greens are called Celadon, and those with purples are called Jun, but essentially they are the same glazes and the same process: the way the potter manipulates the space around the vessel in the kiln is what creates these different results. To spell it out, the pot is the body itself, *jing*, the essential underlying structure; the glaze which bubbles out from the surface is *qi*, the animation of our essential nature; and *shen* is the atmosphere around the pot, the pressure, the dynamic space which determines the ultimate appearance of the vessel!

Mind Training in the Theater

Martial enlightenment, to coin a term, is a major theme of Chinese opera. It is found, for instance, in the epic *Journey to the North*, about the god Xuanwu (Mysterious Warrior), who becomes "empty" when his internal organs are removed. In fact, the notion that heroes fight their way to enlightenment is a guiding organizational principle of the major epics of Chinese theater, like *Canonization of the Gods, Journey to the West,* and *Outlaws of the Marsh.*

The very drums and gongs which are the soundscape of Chinese opera were traditionally part of martial training. The capacity to embody rhythm is itself a demonstration of relaxed focus; the ability to play complex rhythms is evidence of long hours of disciplined awareness.

Drums and gongs were used to deepen operant conditioning, especially as a trigger for developing percussive and explosive movement. And, of course, they were used to send signals and keep troops in order. As a traditional saying goes, "To defend a village, you need a drum and a gong."

In the theater, being able to drop one's identity and take on the physicality, words, history, and appearance of another is an everyday practice—though not all actors develop this capacity. The theater traditions of Asia hold out the possibility of discarding the social self. The religious customs surrounding the theater traditions of Asia are built around emptying the body of habitual limitation and letting go of identity. All five types of martial-arts mind training were traditionally used in the theater to achieve these results.

Embedded Performance Skills

Performance skills are embedded in the movement training of martial arts. Probably the most important of these—and the most difficult to learn—is the ability to hold a shape or a stance. The stances used in martial arts are the basis for the development of the expressiveness of the hands and the voice in theatrical traditions. They are essentially character platforms. In Chinese opera the voice is developed from these stances; movement training is part of voice training. For instance, Chinese opera performers practice handstands, bridges, and kicks to develop their body's capacity for vocal skills. The hands are likewise always trained *on* a stance; they are moved by *shenfa*, the movement dynamics of the torso.

Stance training actually changes the student's body. Stances transform underlying structure and improve efficiency; necessary ingredients for both types of movement. This training has a dual function, however; it is a core element of both theater and martial arts. Trained stances are extremely effective for self-defense. Many people mistakenly imagine that stances are positions which are *fought from*, but in practice, they form a base of body shapes that can be *fought to*. In the event of an attack, fighting to a stance is a way to recover control against chaotic forces and confusion, particularly at close range, when caught off balance, or when attacked from behind—which is the way most surprise attacks happen. Fighting to an upright stance that has been ingrained into the body is a way to regain orientation, and is the basis for taking control of spinning momentum.

Moving with good structure from stance to stance—often called "keeping a frame"—gives movement power and can disorient an attacker. But this is also the physical basis of expressing and maintaining character onstage. One of the ways a performer stays in character is by maintaining a particular stance or repeatedly returning to it. These stances had to be second nature, because Chinese theater performances traditionally lasted for many hours.

The hand shapes and arm positions of martial arts are drilled into students relentlessly and precisely. The same method is used to teach mime, where precisely trained exaggerated movements are used to communicate everyday gestures and actions. Chinese theater uses very few props and almost no stage scenery. Full-body gestures function as a type of sign language denoting specific objects or ideas, which are recognizable to audience members within a given story. In many of the theater traditions of Asia, an outstretched arm with the thumb up can signify that the performer is holding a bow, and two fingers outstretched can signify a sword. This is similar to Euro-American pantomime in that it requires exact body positions that can be dropped and returned to instantaneously; pantomime, however, is focused on creating illusions, and rarely uses the Asian convention of mime as sign language.

The feeling of training in Asian traditions of mime feels identical to training in Chinese martial arts. Holding a position for a long period of time; being tested, corrected, and adjusted by a teacher—perhaps with a slap on the shoulder or pressure against the forearm—is like pounding the body into a mold. It creates the ability to instantly find a body shape or position—so that, for example, the performer can stoop to pet an imaginary dog, and the animal will always appear to be the same height because the hand knows where it is supposed to go relative to the whole body stance. This same training shows the body where to be so that when a performer is pouring an imaginary pitcher of her vanquished enemy's blood into an imaginary cup made out of the top of his skull, it doesn't look like she's spilled it all over the stage. (Try this at home; if you already have traditional martial arts training, this theatrical ability can be acquired without much effort.)

Martial-arts routines contain physical theater skills. The same percussive stamp used to generate power for an arm break or to scrape the skin from a mugger's shins cues the action, distracts the eye, announces anger, implies pain, exaggerates power, and creates the "smack" sound of an elbow connecting with a skull in staged combat in a theatrical context.

Many classic Shaolin positions are designed to manipulate the audience's visual focus. For instance, stances are often angled so as to be seen clearly from a distance. Sudden head turns move the audience's visual focus around the stage; furthermore, a turned head, squared shoulders, and a turned-out leg are standard elements used in the theater to create the illusion of facing someone on the stage while making it easier for the audience to see the performer's whole body. This same physicality is also handy for learning how to get one's entire body off the line of an attack.

Shaolin skills that allow one to appear bigger, smaller, thinner, fatter, closer, or further away are useful in the theater. Elements which function to manipulate the perception of an opponent are useful in both realms. For instance, rounding the back, bending the knees, and tilting the head upward are used to portray servants, comics, and grannies because they make one appear deceptively small and submissive.

Because most martial-arts forms are naturally entertaining ready-made performances, it is relatively easy for martial arts schools to put on shows. Similarly, two-person routines and flow patterns are the traditional tools used to create stage combat routines. Two people who know the same interlocking patterns can quickly improvise a fight scene. Real fighting ability makes staged combat more exciting to watch (as Jackie Chan has proven over and over again). Two-person routines teach timing, distancing, positioning, spatial awareness, superior angles, and a host of other great martial skills.

Acrobatic moves like high kicks, flips, cartwheels, barrel turns, and butterfly kicks are impressive on the stage, but they are also excellent ways of regaining control of the momentum in a self-defense situation where the person being attacked is taking damage. Attackers want to dominate and assert control so they can cause more damage. A powerful way to break that control is to add massive amounts of momentum. Experience with acrobatic moves and long extensions of the limbs also allows a defender to take advantage of nearby walls, trees, and furniture to reverse the power dynamics, neutralize the threat, and escape.

The core of Chinese theatrical training is in the four arts *(sigong)* and the five skills *(wufa)*. The four arts are *chang* (singing), *nian* (reciting), *zuo* (choreography), and da (martial and acrobatic arts). The five skills are "hand" *(shou)*, "eye" *(yan)*, "body" *(shen)*, "method" *(fa)*, and "step" *(bu)*.[6] Modern martial artists study all these except singing and reciting.

---

6   Yung Sai-shing, "Moving Body: The Interactions Between Chinese Opera and Action Cinema." In *Hong Kong Connections, Transnational Imagination in Action Cinema.* Hong Kong University Press, 2005, pp. 27-28.

"Body" and "method" should be read as a single term, *shenfa*, or art of the body—these movements of the whole torso are one of the key markers of a well-trained martial artist.

Embedded Stories

Martial and performing skills are not mutually exclusive. The older the style is, the more theatricality it is likely to have.

As mentioned above, Guan Gong, the god of war, is a well-known character in Chinese theater. He uses a quasi-magical halberd called a *guandao* (war knife) or a *dadao* (great knife) as a weapon *(see cover image)*. This was a real weapon, but was probably used on horseback, not usually wielded at ground level. In the traditional theater of China, they mimed horses rather than bring them on the stage. A *guandao* wielded on the ground is more closely connected to storytelling traditions than it is to combat.

Many martial arts forms tell a story, but in most cases the story has been lost. However, if you know the stories and characters that were once popular, fragments of these stories can be discerned in the theatrical elements of a given form. Theater is the source of many of the names of forms and individual movements within forms. Some examples of movement names include "Monk Clears His Sleeves," from Shaolin; "Thief Steals the Money," from *liuhexinyi*; and "Jade Maiden Works the Shuttles," from *taijiquan*. Shaolin form names are usually theatrical. Erlong is a god character who has three eyes and a pet hellhound; Mulan is the woman warrior made world famous by Disney; Five Tiger Sword is a reference to five demon warriors in a collection of plays called *Canonization of the Gods*. The conventions for naming forms and movements come from theatrical rituals collected in books like *Journey to the West, Outlaws of the Marsh*, and *Journey to the North*.

The close relationship between naming and theater was evident in the storyteller's art as well. Solo storytellers used a percussion instrument called a "clacker" while telling a story; they acted out the fighting moves, naming the moves; and inserted the swishing, splattering, smashing, and clanging sounds of battle into their tales.[7]

Most forms also start in a theatrical way that recalls the opening of an imaginary door or a curtain—stepping over a threshold and

---

7   See Paize Keulemans "Listening to the Printed Martial Arts Scene: Onomatopoeia and the Qing Dynasty Storyeller's Voice," in the *Harvard Journal of Asiatic Studies*, Vol. 67, No. 1 (June 2007), pp. 51-87.

Figure 3. Monk Clears His Sleeves (stance), author, 2016. Photo: Sarah Halverstadt.

loudly stamping the ground. The stage door in Chinese theater is called the Ghost Gate. Stamping is often used in rituals in the same way firecrackers are: to wake demon servants, frighten off ghosts, and to lure troublesome-spirits for capture and imprisonment in a well. As I explain in detail later in this book, most theater in China served the dual purpose of being both entertainment and functioning as a ritual exorcism. Martial-arts forms often conform to the same logic.

Most forms also contain presentation stances of the character being performed. Even if the character being played in a given martial-arts form is unclear, it is often apparent that someone is "taking the stage" in a righteous stance which displays martial prowess. In some styles, like Eight Immortals *(baxian)*, the characters "taking the stage" are obviously the eight immortals, religious figures about whom numerous plays have been written. There is a close parallel here to Chinese theatrical conventions in which a new lead character is presented for the audience's appraisal when first entering the stage. Beijing opera performances are essentially staged just like martial arts forms: a given scene in a play is defined by a performer moving from one stance to another.

The first *lanshouquan* form I learned from my teacher George Xu ends with the mimed actions of catching hold of a horse.

These movements have clear martial techniques associated with them, but they also mime actions. A possible explanation for their origins is found in southern Shanxi province, where there was a ritual performance called "Stealing a Horse," which tells the story of Guan Gong (Guandi) stealing a horse. While *lanshouquan* is not tied directly to any ritual that I know of, these sorts of village ritual performances were commonplace, and given that Guan Gong is known for his martial prowess, we can conclude that these sorts of ritual performances were martial-arts displays.

Chinese martial arts can all be characterized in terms of the theatrical role types they are performing. Characters who are bandits use a broadsword called a *dao*, whereas characters who belong to the gentry or who have exorcist powers use a double-edged straight sword called a *jian*. The basic fighting character role types can be comic, old, young, male, female, monks, priests, generals, bandits, enlightened beings, demons, and even animals. Figuring out the story of the character role portrayed in a particular form or style can explain why that character is acting violently. Martial arts forms have moral lessons or ironic backstories, even if we don't know what they are. For Monkey Style kung fu, the backstory is the epic *Journey to the West*, in which the character Sun

Wukong is fighting his way to enlightenment, unleashing chaos where ever he goes. Similarly, Shaolin staff forms are obviously used for portraying monks, some of them fighting righteous battles; while others are no doubt extricating themselves from ill-advised nights of drinking, gambling and illicit sex, as in the collection of plays called *Crazy Ji, the Mad Monk*.[8][9]

Theatricality in Chinese martial arts is easy to find. It is built into the martial skills we develop. It is found in the righteous characters we strive to become, the mind training we achieve, the performance skills we express, and the stories we tell. Likewise, religion is also easy to find in the martial arts. We train with morality in mind. Mind training is built into martial skills, indeed the types of mind training that are characteristic of Asian religious practice are deeply embedded in martial training. The specific theatrical physicality of Chinese martial skill tells a story which is religious in nature, and as we shall see in the coming chapters, the transformation of the body through martial training is both a religious act and an expression of a specific religious world-view.

Now that we have looked at the ways in which religion and theater are embedded in martial skills, we will take a sharp turn and view things from a completely different perspective. In the next chapter we will look at how martial skills and religion are an essential part of theater.

---

8   Meir Shahar, *Crazy Ji: Chinese Religion and Popular Literature.* Vol. 48. Harvard University Press, 1998.
9   Guo Xiaoting. *Adventures of the Mad Monk Ji Gong.* Trans. John Robert Shaw. Into. Victoria Cass. Tuttle, 2014.

Figure 4. Catching a Horse (stance) author, 2016. Photo: Sarah Halverstadt.

哪吒

Figure 5. Nezha riding fire wheels. Ping Sien Si, Pasir Panjang, Perak, Malaysia, 2014. Photo by Ananjoti (Photo Dharma), Creative Commons, Courtesy of Wikimedia Commons.

Martial Theater

Operatic Warfare

This chapter will examine how martial skills and religion existed in theater. While people generally have some sense that martial arts are intertwined with theatricality, many maintain a strong resistance to the idea; it is as if they don't want to know. Once a comprehensive picture of the possible origins of Chinese martial arts has been presented, it will become clear why this attitude exists.

Anyone who has read one of the epic Chinese "novels," such as *Journey to the West*, will have noticed that the narrative structure of these works is at times difficult to follow, with seemingly irrelevant side stories, repetition, and too many characters to keep track of. This is because these epics were not written as literature; they are collections of rituals. Each individual ritual was a self-contained play, and each collection includes about a hundred plays. In assembling the epics, an attempt was made to link them together with narrative through-lines, but it is rough going. Each epic collection is constructed around one long exorcism, in which demonic-aggressive-chaotic characters are set free to play and commit violent acts. Over the course of the narratives, these characters gradually become more righteous; they become heroes, servants of goodness and order. Their demonic natures are exorcised through acts of merit.

In historic China, highly skilled performances of these classic narratives were staged using real battlefield combat skills. These rituals of theatrical violence were major religious events. A prime example is a type of theater called *zaju*, first written about during the Yuan dynasty (1271–1368), which sometimes included actual army generals performing theatrical roles on the stage. While there are only a few early examples documented, these plays later developed into a common type of ritual for the canonization of gods, which integrated theater and warfare directly. The major Chinese epics—*Journey to the West, Outlaws of the Marsh*, and *Three Kingdoms*—were created by compiling local versions of these canonization rituals.

They are called canonization rituals because there is a parallel with the way the Catholic church has incorporated native gods of places like Haiti and Brazil into its pantheon of saints. In Chinese culture, a family member who has died in battle cannot be incorporated into the ancestral-altar. This means they cannot be "fed" as an ancestor, and are at risk of becoming a wandering ghost. Those who died in battle, especially enemy leaders, became baleful spirits seeking to inspire revenge among the vanquished and disempowered. Generally speaking, in Chinese cosmology, baleful spirits were considered the root cause of violence. If not given a resting place, they would seek to inhabit wild animals, grasses, rocks, and trees, from which they could launch attacks on the living.

Thus, canonization rituals were used to incorporate battlefield dead, and executed enemy leaders, into the theatrical histories and religious cosmologies of the conquering polity. Large public altars or shrines would be built to honor the battlefield dead, house their baleful spirits, and appease their surviving families.

These ritual plays served several other purposes as well. They were performed before battle to invoke demonic forces in the service of human troops. There were several variants of this, including forces visualized in the air above the battle, those imagined fighting alongside militia members, and those who possessed the bodies of soldiers during combat. Naturally, both sides in a conflict could invoke these unseen forces.

In times of peace, these same ritual plays were performed at regular intervals on the festival calendar, and were used to maintain and renew the basis for village militias to fight in ordered unison. How exactly this happened is not well understood, but apparently individuals took on the fighting characteristics of heroes like the Monkey King and Guan Gong. Whole militias may have been grouped according to sworn allegiances that took place within the plays. These festivals were also an opportunity to practice coordinated drills and establish hierarchies of command.

Regularly watching and participating in ritual theater gave people a sense of shared history and purpose, while creating an opportunity to build regional alliances, solve problems, and allocate resources.

Mark Meulenbeld's book *Demonic Warfare* is a superb exploration of canonization literature. While covering a large range of contexts and eras, he focuses on Daoist thunder rituals and a collection of ritual plays called *The Canonization of the Gods (Fengshen Yanyi)*, which was very popular before the twentieth century.

The hero of *Canonization of the Gods* is Nezha, a child-god who is a powerful fighter and the designated protector of the city of Beijing. Nezha is the leader of eight thunder gods who were charged with protecting the eight gates of Beijing. Each of them rides a magical fire-wheel. These characteristics have remarkable parallels to the internal martial art known as *baguazhang* (eight trigrams palm). For example, the walk used to perform *baguazhang* mimes riding a fire-wheel around in circles. The open palm, especially a shaking palm, used in *baguazhang* is a symbol, or *mudra*, used for invoking thunder in both Indian dance and Chinese rituals.[10] With a slight variation, the same *mudra* depicts a drum called a *damaru*, which makes the sound of thunder; and is also used for holding the *vajra* in Tibetan rituals.[11] [12] *(See Figures 6 & 7.)*

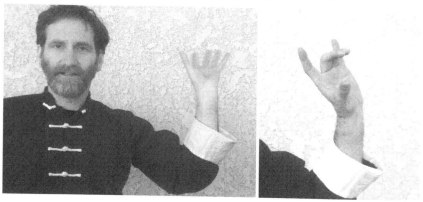

Figure 6. Thunder Mudra, shaking hand, 2016. Photo: Sarah Halverstadt.

Figure 7. Damaru Mudra (South Asian Drum), shaking hand, 2016. Photo: Sarah Halverstadt.

Nezha was invoked as a possessing deity by those who fought during the Boxer Rebellion (1898–1900); several famous masters of *baguazhang* participated in those battles. One of the most famous *baguazuang* master living at the time, Cheng Tinghua, is said to have died battling German soldiers on the streets of Beijing.

10   The Chinese term for *mudra* is *shouyin*.
11   The Sanskrit term *vajra* is *dorjé* in Tibetan and *jingang* in Chinese. The concept means thunder, diamond, and the hardest substance. By inference it means truth, reality, supreme martial prowess, and a deity associated with those qualities.
12   *Vajra* means both thunder and, as will be explained in the subsequent chapter on Shaolin, an impenetrable martial-arts body.

There are also common *baguazhang* styles called "swimming dragon," and "snake style." The creation story of Nezha has him fighting and defeating dragons in the ocean, and he is known as a subduer of snakes. He is often depicted with eight arms and a dragon skin draped over his shoulders.

Baguazhang also uses the same specialized weapons used by Nezha: The two-headed spear and a "thunder hoop" (sometimes called the wind-fire wheel, *see figure 8)*. In addition, *baguazhang* uses a giant broadsword, and sometimes a giant straight sword, too (they are comically giant because Nezha is a little child, so everything he picks up looks big). And lastly, Nezha kills dragons, and Chinese dragons have deer horns, so *baguazhang* has another weapon called deer horns, possibly inspired by magical weapons from India.

While the exact historic relationship between the martial art of *baguazhang* and the historic canonization ritual plays of Nezha is obscure, the numerous parallels between the two make the possibility of a common origin remarkably strong.

The Pervasiveness of Theater

Theater in China was pervasive. Before the twentieth century, it was everywhere. Whether people were watching it, listening to it, or participating in it, theater was the most common form of entertainment in cities, villages, and pilgrimage sites. It was in the streets, in the rivers, on lakes, in temples, set up in open fields, and in people's homes. And it wasn't just a form of entertainment; it was the most common and widespread experience of public religion. Chinese theater—that is, professional theater, usually referred to in English as Chinese opera—was commonly called "Putting on a show for the gods."

China was full of temples, too. In fact, rather than talking about Chinese popular religion, it might be more accurate to talk about temple culture or temple religion, because so much of Chinese society was organized around temples. Temples weren't just dedicated to Buddhism, Daoism, or Confucianism; they were also dedicated to specific gods, both local and national, of which there were hundreds. People didn't belong to only one temple or make offerings to a single god; they made offerings to many gods in many different temples, and larger temples usually had multiple gods.

It was very common for temples to have a stage for theater; in fact, it wasn't unusual for provincial centers to have as many as two

Figure 8. Author with Two Headed Spear, Nezha's hoop, and standing on an imaginary wind-fire wheel, 2016. Photo: Sarah Halverstadt.

Figure 9. Doing Baguazhang with Nezha's Wind-Fire Wheels, 2016. Photo: Sarah Halverstadt.

Figure 10. The child god Nezha with a Big Bagua Sword, 2016. Photo: Sarah Halverstadt.

Figure 11. Dragon Prince, with horns, Nezha's enemy. From *The Dragon, Image, and Demon; or, The Three Religions of China*, by Hampden C. DuBose. London, S. W. Partridge and Co. 1886. Courtesy of the Internet Archive.

Figure 12. Bagua with Deer Horns, wrestling a dragon? 2016. Photo: Sarah Halverstadt.

hundred permanent stages. But professional theater troupes were quite capable of putting on more minimalist productions. Technically, all that was needed was a large piece of red felt, which could be rolled out anywhere. Performances on boats or barges were common too. For larger productions or festivals, massive stages and full sets of bleachers could be quickly put together out of bamboo scaffolds. Theater was everywhere.

Figure 13. Bamboo Scaffolding, ~1900. Image courtesy of Peter Lockhart Smith and Historical Photographs of China, University of Bristol.

In urban areas, there were of course full-scale theaters that ran shows all year long; in fact, many cities had a whole district dedicated to theater. These districts were called "scholar towns," as they were technically outside of official city limits and were continuously packed with large numbers of students in need of distraction from the Sisyphean struggle of trying to pass the imperial exams in the hope of getting a government appointment.

The elite gentry and literati were huge fans and patrons of the theater. In fact, owning a performing troupe or even a single actor was a huge status symbol, perhaps a bit like owning a Porsche or a home theater system would be today. Theater performances inside the homes and gardens of the well-to-do were a central focus of social life.

There were other types of professional festival and street performers as well—acrobats, strongmen, magicians, storytellers, puppeteers, and performers putting on all sorts of displays of martial prowess. The basic training for all of these skills was martial arts. Of course, terms like "strongman" and "magician" are modern—the skill sets and tricks of these street performers overlapped: acrobats did magic and storytellers used puppets. This is probably the best explanation for why there are hundreds of different styles of martial arts out there. (One time, while visiting a puppet museum in Taiwan, I struck up a conversation with a puppet master, explaining a bit about my interests. He smiled, reached over to turn on some music, and then dropped into a perfect horse stance with a puppet on each hand. For the next three minutes I watched two bandits curse each other and fight over which was better, Wudang or Shaolin.)

Amateur performers constituted another whole category. One of the reasons the literati kept theater performers in their homes was that they would study with them for fun. If these literati got good at a role, they would sometimes perform for their friends and family alongside their hired performers. Drinking establishments and restaurants often had professional performers around who could be hired to perform for a table, or accompany a customer if they wished to sing. This could easily turn into a competition amongst the whole group, where each guest was required to try their hand at a classic theatrical role, perform a physical feat like breaking chopsticks on their throat, or offer up some other form of entertainment.

Theater performers living in the home were sometimes under contract, and at other times were bought outright like bonded servants, or even slaves. They taught anyone in the home who wanted to learn, especially children (it is far easier to impart intensely demanding physical training to children). Much of this training was devoted to singing, but all professional actors were fully trained in the movement basics of martial arts.

Most people could not afford to buy or hire an actor to live in their home, but people from all levels of society found ways to study with theater professionals, making amateur theater groups more common than professional troupes. Learning to perform was itself a common source of entertainment.

Most of what we have been discussing so far falls into the category of Chinese opera. But there were many other types of popular theater. During large festivals the statues of the gods from the surrounding temples would be carried to the large outdoor theater and put in seats as honored guests. Chinese gods are often thought to have some lingering human appetites; since everyone likes theater, the thinking went, the gods must too. That's why they called theatrical performances "Putting on a show for the gods." The process of carrying the gods to the temple was an elaborate affair, and probably unique to each locale.

One version, involving young men collectively called Songjian troops, has been well documented in Taiwan and is experiencing a revival. In this ceremony, young men were initiated as the guards of a martial temple god. These young men were socially marginal rough types, the kind of jolly men who like to fight and get in trouble, yet who could be enlisted to help protect the village or chase after bandits. These initiates of the martial temple would be trained in fighting skills and would learn specific martial dances for transporting the statues of a martial god like Guan Gong. The training process also involved making offerings (often of alcohol) at the altar of the god, wearing talismans, and going into altered states of consciousness to learn from the god directly. Before bringing the god out, the initiates would fast and refrain from sex and other taboo activities. The day before the procession they would sleep in the temple and then put on costumes and makeup, after which they were forbidden to speak. Each of eight or ten young men would become a different "demon general." These "generals" were all dangerous demons who had been converted to righteous conduct in service of the god, and each carried a symbolic magical torture weapon.

The journey carrying the god from the temple to the stage could take days; the procession would be accompanied by other ritual specialists and musicians playing gongs and drums. Along the way the young men would dance in magical martial patterns, and when they passed a business or a home they would enter and do a purification to chase off ghosts, using firecrackers and a magical stepping pattern called the "Big Dipper Step."

Other Songjian troops would be carrying other martial gods from other temples to the stage at the same time, so there was a chance two groups could meet. Because the other Songjian troops performing were actually the same demon generals, if two like demons saw each other they would have to fight. The combatants in these fights were trance-mediums channeling the demon general, when they are done fighting they fall backwards into the waiting arms of their friends with no memory of the incident.

The Songjiang troops are just one example of a widespread phenomenon. Ritual societies of amateur performers that used martial arts movements as part of their basic training were everywhere, locally unique in their characteristics and extremely diverse in their purposes. These did not necessarily have any connection to staged theater. Lion dances are a good example. These are always performed by trained martial artists, who use drums, gongs, and firecrackers to frighten away demonic forces. Lion dances are still commonly used today for celebrations and for announcing the opening of a new business.

The subject of community rituals and festivals is incredibly complex precisely because it is so diverse. China's ancient and complex liturgical calendar, the *Tongshu*, is one of the oldest continuously published books on earth. It incorporates numerous historic local ritual calendars that designate the relationships between people, the land, rivers, natural cycles, and the gods.

There was a vast array of different types of ritual experts who specialized in maintaining and renewing these dynamic relationships between the seen and unseen worlds. These included shamans, spirit mediums, those who channeled the dead, those who regulated the weather, healers, those who warded off harmful forces, talisman makers, those who mediated conflicting interests, and those that alleviated the sense of injustice and suffering in the world with visions of other worlds, other dimensions, and other times. Such work had major theatrical aspects, even as it was deeply religious. All of it included aspects of myth-making and storytelling.

Buddhism, Daoism, and Confucianism intertwined with ritual temple culture in every imaginable variation. Sometimes a temple was organized exclusively around one set of religious doctrines, like Daoism, and sometimes there was no discernible doctrine at all. There is a ritual in Southern China that takes place once every ten years and lasts ten days, in which the ritual masters switch back and forth between wearing Buddhist hats and wearing Daoist hats, and in so doing switch genders—the Daoist priests in this case being female and *yin*, the Buddhists being male and *yang*. There are rituals from Shanxi province which have no evidence of Buddhist or Daoist doctrine but instead include ritual specialists called "Yinyang masters" who are experts at, among other things, *fengshui* and divination. Rituals could include headmen playing theatrical roles while wearing masks handed down from generation to generation, or handed from family to family in a rotating or divined cycle. Rituals often included various types of martial processions or theatrical enactments of capturing tigers or demons, conquering enemies or surviving plague and famine. The permutations were endless.

While it might be going too far to say that all ritual theatricality involved in-depth physical training, the movement of ritual specialists was in fact a demonstration of self-cultivation and moral conduct. Indicative of the connection between martial arts and ritual experts is the little-known fact that the term used to describe the many years of training for a Daoist priest in Fujianese was *"kung fu"*—the same term that became popular worldwide for describing Chinese martial arts in the twentieth century.

The Pervasiveness of Violence

One of the questions people often ask me when they hear that I think theater and martial arts were a single subject is, "But could all those theater people really fight? Isn't the training for theater different from that of martial arts? Doesn't the purpose of the training make a big difference in the results?" —Well, yes, and no.

One of the weapons used by numerous Chinese martial arts systems is a small wooden bench. These bench-fighting techniques are real. Because violence was pervasive, people learned to fight with everything in their environment. But using a wooden bench is also theatrical; a whole solo routine done with a bench is comic, and was meant to be seen that way. It seems unlikely that anyone chasing after a group of bandits would intentionally choose a wooden bench as a weapon, and that is exactly why it is so amusing when a performer does it on the stage. (As a general rule, if you can think of something you would never want to have happen to you, you can be sure that someone else would like to see it on the stage.) Two-person routines *(duifang taolu)* also train real skills that are readily adaptable to theatrical presentations. In my own work, I have found two-person martial-arts routines to be a great base for improvising scenes and dialogue.

In times before police with radios, modern prisons, and an effective government monopoly on violence, people lived with violence around every corner. The modern world has so much food, safe shelter, education, and ways to get rich that interpersonal violence and crimes of desperation are a tiny fraction of what they once were. Generally speaking, the past everywhere was extremely violent. That's why, all over the world, people have developed ways of fighting and ways of passing on those skills from generation to generation. Even putting warfare aside, pre-modern China was an extremely violent place. Some other genres of martial arts will be discussed later in this book, but it is hard to find a place on earth which has the variety, complexity, and continuity of China's martial-arts forms.

For most of history, China was wealthier than the rest of the world. It was a large country with an effective network of rivers and roads. Keeping those roads and rivers open for commerce and the movement of men-at-arms was essential for the survival of China's central governments. Beginning as far back as the Tang Dynasty (618-907) the Chinese government began using cavalries to put down rebellions. The cavalries were not ethnically Chinese (Han), they were made up of Mongolian and Hui peoples mostly from the North and North-Western borders. These cavalries were moved around the country to hotspots of conflict in order to hold the empire together.

Garrison towns were governed under a national military *(wu)* code. Because these towns were outside the control of provincial magistrates, jurisdictional disputes were common—a boon for small time banditry. The archaic patchwork of ancient provincial boundaries along with the military boundaries created an opportunity for bandits who could often escape capture by crossing into another jurisdiction.[13]

Each province was managed by a single magistrate, who, after success on a very competitive exam and often after years of waiting for an appointment, was assigned to a province far from his home. Each magistrate had a small personal staff of unpaid servants called *yamen* runners, who executed warrants, extracted confessions and kept the jails. *Yamen* made their living by extracting bribes in exchange for favorable treatment. Theoretically a magistrate had enormous power and authority; however, there was only one magistrate for even the

13   Joseph Esherick, *The Origins of the Boxer Uprising.* Univ of California Press, 1988.

largest of provinces, and outside of the provincial capitals, most crime and moral corruption was dealt with locally through clan networks and village headmen. Personal safety was precarious because it was a function of the patronage networks each individual belonged to. In order to combat organized banditry and rebellion, magistrates mainly relied on the aid and martial prowess of headmen and the gentry to assemble and lead men-at-arms.

With lots of valuables traveling the rivers and roads, banditry was rife. Bandit armies and bandit networks were everywhere. Bandit leaders were constantly assessing whether it would be more advantageous to rob people on the roads or to extort local officials and merchant networks for the privilege of using roads through bandit-controlled territory. Government officials, on the other hand, had to weigh the benefits that might come from making alliances with bandit armies to put down rebellions against the costs of dedicating resources to hunting down bandits who had become too much of a burden on local commerce and too great a threat to local order.

Beyond banditry, violence had other causes. Whenever commerce was disrupted or crops failed, people starved—and starving people tend to do desperate, violent things. Even in the best of times, roads were dangerous and cities were walled for defense. High-quality weapons were everywhere. Although weapons were technically illegal within the walls of cities like Beijing, which had over a million inhabitants by the year 1500, the daily count of confiscated weapons like cudgels, knives, swords, whips, chains, and so on suggests violent crime was rampant. Kidnapping was also a common problem, especially of children, who could be captured in one part of China and sold in another.[14]

During the late imperial period, there was a legal category called "bare-sticks," which was a lewd reference to unmarried, unattached men. It is estimated that some twenty-five percent of adult men belonged to the bare-sticks category at any given time. (Marriage markets were tight because wealthy men could take multiple wives; furthermore, both men and women were expected to bring resources to a marriage, so a lack of resources on either side meant marriages were put off indefinitely.) Bare-sticks received harsher punishments than family men, and were treated unequally by the courts because they were seen as volatile, desperate, and dangerous, and were feared by society. The social anxiety was so high that both Buddhist and Daoist monks were considered bare-sticks

---

14　David Robinson, *Bandits, Eunuchs, and the Son of Heaven, Rebellion and the Economy of Violence in Mid-Ming China.* Honolulu: University of Hawai'i Press, 2001.

in the legal code.[15] Understanding how prevalent bare-sticks were also helps explain why sworn brotherhoods were such a common means of assuring mutual aid and protection.

Historically, China was a dangerous place; everyone had experience with violence, and relied on the immediate protection offered within social hierarchies and families. These immediate allies were in turn part of a complex of alliances between ever-larger circles of power. It was in this violent context, then, that theater developed and thrived as both a central focus and a wanted distraction in people's lives.

Training as Play

Historically, Chinese children lived in a dangerous world where the possibility of kidnapping and other types of extreme violence was ever-present. It was also a world where the theatrical mode of expression was fully integrated into both the entertainment and the educational, moral, religious milieus they participated in. Anyone teaching martial arts to children knows that they will fall into play without any prompting. It seems reasonable to assume that children in the past played with martial arts a lot. And why not? Play is among the best ways of learning, because it imprints or conditions skills and abilities unconsciously so that they become spontaneously available. People who wrestle a lot as children, for example, have easy access to those skills as adults. The same is true for any skills that are integrated into play.

It therefore follows that adults who want their children to have martial skills will attempt to transmit them to children through play. Developing martial prowess as a form of play allows for the complete integration of music, fighting, acting, improvisation, creative movement patterns, problem-solving, testing, fostering the imagination, and exploring moral questions and situational conundrums. If we consider the experiences of religion and theater in China we see that they have always been a fundamental part of martial arts.

Adults can also learn through play, but getting them to play isn't always so easy. The realm of sworn brotherhoods was one place where adults did learn through play. Sworn brotherhoods were both inspired by and a major subject of plays performed by professionals and amateurs alike. The epic stories *Outlaws of the Marsh, Three Kingdoms, Canonization*

---

15 David Ownby, "Approximations of Chinese Bandits: Perverse Rebels, Romantic Heroes, or Frustrated Bachelors?." *Chinese Femininities/Chinese Masculinities: A Reader* (2002): 226-251.

of the Gods, and *Journey to the North* are all narratives built around sworn brotherhoods. Sworn brotherhoods often took their names or initiation rituals from similar events in the theater. Discussing violence in terms of *play* is somewhat taboo, and I suspect that writings about real-life sworn brotherhoods, both in historic China and more recent scholarship, may be missing some of the play implicit in their rituals of bonding.

Take, for example, Daniel Amos' writing on Triad culture in Hong Kong.[16] He describes small groups of young men who have received secret transmissions going back twenty-four generations, rituals which take them into trances as various characters from popular theater and religion. They become possessed by these deities and act out all sorts of improvised routines. The non-possessed members put questions to those possessed by the gods, and gods pose questions to each other. Inevitably they will get into an argument and come to blows. Thus the monkey king's sidekick Piggy will get in a fight with Guan Gong's son Guan Ping, and they will roll around exchanging blows until a non-possessed onlooker takes the correct ritual actions, perhaps flashing a *mudra (shouyin)* and saying a magic word, to bring them out of their trance. The possessed will fall over backwards, and, if asked, will state that they have no memory of anything that happened to them while in character, even asking questions like, "What god was I?" This improvised fighting sounds like a lot more fun than regular old sparring. The lineage of twenty-four generations may, of course, be exaggerated, but the practice was likely widespread among those in the lower ranks of society. Amos explains that these sorts of bouts functioned in the participants' minds as a kind of preliminary—perhaps even initiatory—experience for young toughs entering at the bottom of the Triads.

The Triads are called Tiandihui (the Heaven-Earth Society) in Chinese. Today they are well-organized criminal organizations. But in times past they were secret societies of mutual aid that occupied a realm halfway between rebellion and banditry. The lines separating mutual aid, defending one's village, banditry, rebellion, dangerous religious cults, and acting tough are sometimes hard to see; before the twentieth century, it depended more on where one was standing than on any objective measures. One suspects the Triads often functioned somewhat like the Freemasons did in the Wild West: people would contact or join them in order to get a job or to solve a local dispute. This seems especially likely where the government was weak or not trusted.

Religion can be funny. The martial gods of popular temple culture

16   Daniel Miles Amos, *Marginality and the Hero's Art: Martial Artists in Hong Kong and Guangzhou (Canton)*. University Microfilms International [Publisher], 1996.

were unruly, sometimes crafty, vengeful, jealous, lustful, or impulsive, and some had a good sense of humor. Functionally, the line between religion and theater did not exist. As we shall see, lazy, impractical gods could be punished!

In his book *History in Three Keys: The Boxers as Event, Experience, and Myth*, Paul A. Cohen explains the way in which Chinese religion could alternate between secular and sacred. Below he discusses the many accounts of people possessed by martial gods of the opera during the Boxer Rebellion in 1898–1900. Thousands of Chinese

were killed by organized groups of Boxers (Yihequan, or "fighters united in harmony") who believed they were bulletproof:

> [T]he sharp boundaries between the "secular" and the "sacred," to which modern Westerners are accustomed, simply did not exist. The gods of popular religion were everywhere and "ordinary people were in constant contact" with them...People depended on them for protection and assistance in time of need. But when they failed to perform their responsibilities...they [could] be punished..."If the god does not show signs of appreciation of the need of rain," Arthur Smith wrote toward the end of the nineteenth century, "he may be taken out into the hot sun and left there to broil, as a hint to wake up and do his duty." This...matter-of-fact attitude Chinese typically displayed toward their deities doubtless contributed to the widespread view among Westerners...that the Chinese were not an especially religious people. It would be more accurate, I believe to describe the fabric of Chinese social and cultural life as being permeated through and through with religious beliefs and practices.
>
> ...[T]he martial arts, healing practices, and the heroes of popular literature and opera often inhabit a space in Chinese culture that seems unambiguously "secular." But it is not at all unusual, as clearly suggested in the accounts of Boxer spirit possession...for these selfsame phenomena to be incorporated into a fully religious framework of meaning.[17]

17   Paul Cohen, *History in Three Keys: The Boxers as Event, Experience, and Myth*. New York: Columbia University Press, 1997, p.102.

The group known as the Boxers (Yihequan) had its origins in Plum-flower Fist (Meihua Quan), a playful, festive, multi-village organization that was created in response to real suffering in a violent world. The group derived its name from the gatherings in early spring to celebrate the plum blossoms. At these gatherings people from different villages would gather to share food, perform their martial arts, have friendly matches, watch musical theater, and practice storytelling.

Plum Flower Fist was sometimes called Plum-flower Religion (Meihua Jiao). Like government and theater, this institution was divided into two parts: a civil *(wen)* branch and a martial *(wu)* branch. The civil branch read scriptures and practiced things we would be more likely to associate with religion, like curing illnesses via chanting, talismans, and exorcism. The martial branch practiced solo *(taolu)* and two-person *(duifang taolu)* martial-arts forms, and trained for militia, anti-banditry, and crop-guarding work. The purpose of having two branches of the organization was to comply with laws forbidding *under penalty of death* the combination of martial training (weapons and troop training) with millennialist ideologies (historically, most rebellions in China arose through millennialist movements and charismatic cults). In 1897–98, growing conflict caused a group to splinter off from the Plum Flower Society and start an organization under the new name Yihequan (Fighters United in Harmony), known to history as the Boxers.[18]

No discussion of adult play would be complete without mentioning drinking games aimed at breaking down inhibitions. These played a big part in martial culture. It was standard to make offerings of strong liquor at the temples to martial gods; presumably, it was the local toughs who frequented these temples that ended up drinking it.

Many villages had homegrown martial-arts experts who taught family and friends at home or in public spaces. There is a long history of traveling martial-arts experts being offered a place to sleep and teach in a local martial temple. After all, the temples *were* the public spaces. Because martial arts, theater, and religion were linked in the popular imagination, nearly everyone had access to some form of martial arts learning through play. These local and traveling martial-arts experts were also amateur showmen; their real, effective, and practical martial skills were serious business, but they were also experts in a kind of play.

---

18   Esherick 1987: 152–153.

More about Opera

Opera was an integral part of the festival calendar, which varied enormously depending on the unique customs of each locale; and actors were a type of ritual expert, a necessary part of China's martial and religious culture.

The term "Chinese opera" covers a lot of ground. "Chinese" could refer to seven roughly defined dialects, which by some counts can be broken down further into as many as three hundred local speaking styles which linguists call topolects *(fengyan)*. In addition to those, opera used archaic, classical, and poetic forms of speech, as well as the separate languages spoken by various ethnic minorities. "Opera" refers not just to singing technique, spoken language, heightened spoken language, and vocal improvisation, but to acrobatics, contortion, magic, mime, physical theater, stage combat, instrumental music, percussion, and dance. As explained earlier, the "opera" was the primary way most people experienced myths, legends, history, poetry, and classical language. For most people, it was also the primary and most widespread public experience of religion. The main characters embodied on the stage were gods, demons, ghosts, animal spirits, and heroes of the past who had themselves become gods worshiped at temples.

Opera's ritual function, in a broad sense, was to create and renew alliances in both the human and the unseen supernatural worlds.

In the human realm, the cooperative effort of pooling resources from within a village—or multiple villages—to put on a performance was a way of regularly demonstrating and solidifying the commitment to mutual aid. Wealthy or powerful families could also demonstrate their magnanimity by sponsoring an opera. In the unseen realm of gods and demons, the ritual aspects of opera were a way to protect against chaotic forces, like diseases and natural disasters, by maintaining dynamic and reciprocal relationships with local gods, spirits, and ancestors. Operas functioned as offerings, sacrifices, and a form of spiritual contract. Festivals featuring opera were also a key feature of market towns; they were the nexus of commerce, providing the context for a great deal of buying and selling.

Mean People

Given the centrality of opera, it is quite surprising that professional performers were part of a degraded caste called mean people *(jianmin)*, which also included prostitutes and *yamen* runners (who worked as servants, jailers, and muscle for the local magistrate).[19] In the social hierarchy, actors were at rock bottom, beneath beggars and thieves. Professional performers were in this caste in perpetuity; that is, all of their descendants would belong to the caste, and could not marry out. New troupe members were either the children of performers or were formally adopted, often bought from destitute parents. *Jianmin* were forbidden to take military or civil service exams. They were also part of a larger group of outcasts (literally "out" castes) that included some ethnic minorities who were, by decree, required to sleep outside of city or village walls. No matter how wealthy or famous a performer became, he was required to step into the gutter to let even the humblest peasant walk by.

For the most part, opera troupes were regional, and used regional dialects. For instance, there were fourteen distinct styles of opera in and around Canton, each corresponding to one of the regional village communities located there. In the south, some groups called "in-river troupes" would live and travel on boats that carried about a hundred performers and their staff. For big festivals, as many as three boats would arrive. In the areas further north around Nanjing, performances often took place on boats or barges. Out-of-river troupes traveled by road, moving in a circuit between villages, market towns, or pilgrimage sites.

The paradox of being loved as performers on an individual level and hated as a group may be hard for modern people to comprehend (although some Hollywood stars do come to mind). The origins of the opera caste are unknown, but there are a few major theories. Some speculate that they were once part of a distinct ethnic group, possibly originating from Rajasthan in North India, who are known in Europe as Romani. Performing troupes were often sent to the emperor as gifts of tribute by foreign states, so it is also possible that over the centuries opera performers became a composite of many ethnic origins. Yet another possibility is that the first emperor of the Ming dynasty (1368–1644), Zhu Yuanzhang, made all the civil and military officials who had served the previous dynasty, along with their families, into itinerant performers and prostitutes in perpetuity as a punishment for perfidy. In short, opera troupes may have started out as the most educated and physically talented people in the country. It is also possible that such a purge happened in the transitions between earlier dynasties as well.

---

19   *Yamen* runners were unpaid servants who carried the magistrate in palanquins and were in charge of executing warrants, jails, and torturing confessions. They were paid primarily by bribes, generally given in hopes of securing favorable treatment.

Good-looking actors, always on the move from village to village, might have left behind trails of jealousy and illegitimate children (who they could later collect). This could explain the general antipathy toward them, and also might have been a source of regular social violence. In any event, actors everywhere are regarded with suspicion because they make their living pretending to be powerful people. They have a kind of super-power—the ability to manipulate people's perceptions of status and authenticity.

Chinese opera performers were trained for a minimum of seven years—usually longer. First a child would learn a precise stance, and would be made to hold it every day, for as long it took to permanently transform their body. Then they would learn the transition to another stance, and so on and on, until the whole sequence could be practiced as a routine. All actors were trained in bridges, handstands, splits, and the basics of acrobatic martial arts. Around puberty they became specialists in a standard role type.

Troupes were generally all-male or all-female, so each gender played both male and female roles. In the Qing Dynasty (1644–1911) it was technically illegal for women to perform opera, but it is hard to assess the extent to which this was enforced. Besides being divided into male and female categories, they were divided into *wu* (martial) roles such as general, warrior woman, or clown; and *wen* (civil) roles, such as scholar-official, beautiful maiden, or handsome devil. About ten percent of performers were acrobatic, contortionist, animal-role specialists who did stunts and played creatures like pigs, crabs, turtles, dogs, tigers, dragons, and even magical trees.

Before the twentieth century, training was conducted entirely in secret, transmitted from masters to disciples in long lineages. The repertories of these full-time professional troupes could be massive. One version of *Mulian Rescues His Mother* actually took a month to perform in its entirety; and a single play segment often lasted six hours.

Naturally, because they lived outside of city walls and traveled the land of rivers and lakes, opera troupes had to be able to defend themselves. They were often paid in silk, which they used to make costumes and which was a valuable commodity for trade. They carried their belongings and valuables in standard opera chests, an obvious target for bandits. Also, their low caste diminished their credibility in the courts, so they were punished more severely as a matter of law. Performers had an extra incentive to be good at neutralizing attackers without causing permanent damage, which required a higher order of martial skill.

The key terms used in the teaching of Chinese opera are the same as those used in Chinese martial arts, indicating the same processes of body-mind learning. For instance, *yi* (intent), *jing* (essential, underlying self-reproducing structure), *qi* (energy or presence), *shen* (spirit, gods, spatial awareness), and *xu* (emptiness, effortless) are all terms used both in opera and martial arts. Likewise, physical theater and stage combat are high-injury disciplines. For people who relied on their physical prowess and self-healing powers to be able to perform night after night, year after year; the incentives for constant refinement, conditioning, and making the art "internal" were strong.

The basic training for martial artists and theatrical performers was nearly the same, but because professional performers had no other legal option for making a living other than to be in the opera, being good was the only possibility. If they weren't good at acting, they could play the music; if they weren't good at music, they could become stage hands and make-up assistants. If they weren't good at that, they could engage in sex or violence for money, or they could starve.

Stage vs. Combat

Although opera performers had strong incentives to be expert fighters, it is worth considering whether there are real differences between stage combat and real combat.

In the modern era, professional fight choreographers sometimes point to the big differences between what they do and actual fighting. For example, in stage combat, one intentionally telegraphs strikes so that one's partner can see or feel a strike coming—and the audience must see it coming too. In actual fighting, however, the element of surprise is a force multiplier. Both types of training, however, need both types of abilities. In stage combat there are many things the audience is not supposed to see, such as the fact that the punch didn't actually hit anything, and that the sound it seemed to have made was actually a hand slapping the thigh. Stage magic and illusion, including stage combat, are as concerned with what the audience does see as with what it does not see. Similarly, in fighting it is often necessary to "sell a fake"—that is, to set up an intended attack by getting the opponent to see and respond to a false attack. Both arts are fundamentally about managing other people's attention.

Furthermore, the expression "timing is everything" is used in both, because rhythmic training is an essential skill in both arts. And both arts have a great need for accuracy: In stage combat one has to miss by just enough to make it safe, yet have it look real. In a fight, it is essential to accurately target the most vulnerable areas.

Spatial awareness, improvisation, agile kicks, good range of motion, and mastery of whole-body momentum are treasured equally by both types of training. Angles are used differently in the two arts, but both require superb awareness and ability to apply knowledge of angles. Power generation is necessary for doing damage in actual fighting, whereas on the stage explosive power is important for impressive displays, flips, tornado kicks, partner assists, and jumping over people's heads.

In short, theatrical stage combat is just another form of fighting. Crop-guarding requires different skills than police work, which is a different skill-set from self-defense, which is different again from surprise assault, or matched fighting with rules. There is no good substitute for direct experience when establishing skill with any particular type of violence.

Conclusion

The first chapter looked at the ways in which theater and religion are embedded in martial skills. This chapter took a sharp turn and looked at how martial skills and religion are essential elements of Chinese theater. The next chapter will take another sharp turn. This time to look at how theater and martial skills are key to understanding Chinese religions.

The operatic warfare described at the beginning of this chapter is just one small example of the many ways theater, martial skills, and religion were part of a complex whole. In China, the pervasiveness of both violence and theater led to a deep integration of the two. China developed wildly diverse and highly specialized integrations of martial skill. Theater professionals, a wide array of amateur performers, and ritual experts integrated religious concepts and martial skills into what we today call martial arts. The next chapter will look more deeply at the martial and theatrical nature of Chinese religions.

Martial Religions

This chapter will examine theater and martial arts from the perspective of Chinese religion. A central organizing element of Chinese religion is making commitments. Commitments take three major forms: talismans, precepts, and sworn oaths. In Chinese cosmology, human beings are defined by our commitments, as are ghosts, gods, demons, and immortals. Seen from the point of view of Chinese religion, martial arts are the physical equivalent of commitments, which take the form of precepts, talismans, and sworn oaths.

Making strong commitments and keeping them is a way to change one's behavior. Many people in Christian societies would agree with this, but wouldn't necessarily consider commitment a religious issue; however, when those commitments are the Ten Commandments, they certainly would. Chinese religions have created many similarly important lists of precepts, but there is no single doctrine. China also has a tradition of talismans, which function largely by tricking one's unconscious mind into behaving a certain way. Talismans come in countless varieties—images, writing, objects— all of which are symbolic covenants which represent commitments made with the spirit world. Similarly, sworn oaths and sworn brotherhoods are commitments between people, strengthened by covenants with an unseen world.

Defining religion is a tricky business. Anthropologists and experts on comparative religion make do with provisional definitions, because we do not have a convincing, comprehensive definition of religion—still, one might say "you know it when you see it."

Christianity and atheism tend to frame religions reductively as belief systems. This is a kind of information filter which creates big misunderstandings about the rest of the world. Religion in large parts of the world, including historic China, did not require belief. A person does not have to believe that a wealth-producing talisman has magic powers, because simply hiding it under the flap of one's checkbook and making commitments to the god of frugality may be enough to make it work in the right social and aesthetic environment. The word for talisman, *fu*, literally means a contract, and contracts do not require belief.

Martial arts are not built around a belief system; they are built around the religious idea of accumulating merit. Committed actions, contracts if you will, are the primary method of accumulating merit. Fully understood, the term "kung fu" means "meritorious action"; that is, to act through a body which has accumulated merit. From the Chinese cultural point of view, the human ability to make and keep commitments is what makes humans fundamentally different from other animals.

Defining Humanness: Conduct, Appetites and Commitment

Martial skills, in violent eras, were integrated into the religious rituals of daily life. The very words "kung fu" were used to describe the dedications of merit that people made to temple gods—fixing bridges, taking care of children, clearing brush around the river, and training to defend the village. These were all part of the same notion of good works.[20]

The physicality of martial arts, the movement language itself, was used by all the various types of amateur and professional theater. Many of the stepping and running patterns used in martial-arts schools today were used in seasonal ritual processions which went on for days at a time, helping to develop a strong constitution in the youth who performed them. At the end of such a ritual all the "merit" accumulated would be dedicated to a greater good. In abstract terms, that "good" might be a god's blessing on the whole region, but in concrete terms it meant that the youth of the village had more physical prowess to apply to village defense and the hard work of farming, or it meant that the process of putting on a large complex festival required people at all levels of society to organize and cooperate, thus resolving petty conflicts in the process of acquiring merit.

The monastic traditions of Buddhism and Daoism created many elaborate lists of precepts to help groups of monks or nuns, who did not share family bonds, to get along well in closely packed living situations. These include admonitions like clean up after yourself, don't have sex,

---

20   *See* Kristofer Schipper's introduction to *Taoism and the Arts of China*. Edited by Stephen Little and Shawn Eichman. Univ of California Press, 2000.

don't eat garlic, don't make lots of noise, and show up to scheduled events promptly. In a traditional Chinese village, keeping a few simple precepts was a time-honored way of being religious. Memorizing a chant from a morality text, perhaps written by a spirit medium, was a common way for lay Buddhists to reinforce precepts, and short lists of precepts were often created as summaries of sacred texts.

Confucianism and Daoism both have traditions of precepts that predate monastic culture by hundreds of years. Confucian precepts, based on the writings of Confucius and Mencius, are predicated on the notion that it is a lifetime practice to match one's words with one's actions—correct conduct requires a continuous effort. Thus, a popular expression of religion was to commit to a particular precept—say, humility, for instance—and try to get all of one's actions, words, and thoughts to reflect it. Confucian ritual performances relied on the notion that the ritual masters or performers aspired to perfect behavior, in accord with a list of precepts. In practice, village rituals were highly imaginative and varied, mixing Buddhism, Daoism, Confucianism, and local cults freely, but inherent to all of these traditions is the idea that one is defined by the commitments one keeps (or breaks).

The role of Daoism in the creation of martial arts is a very large subject with countless possible points of entry. One way in is to examine early Daoist precepts and consider how they may have inspired people with martial skills. Here are the nine Xiang'er Daoist precepts from the first century CE:[21]

Practice:

- Honesty
- Weakness and flexibility
- Femininity
- Emptiness
- Freedom from desire
- Stillness
- Kindness and generosity
- Being good at completing things
- Not-doing *(wuwei)*

This list was created as a summary of the *Daodejing*, Daoism's most sacred text. These precepts are guidelines for Daoist conduct. Each

---

21   Bokenkamp, Stephen R., and Peter S. Nickerson. *Early Daoist Scriptures.* Vol. 1. Univ of California Press, 1997.

precept can be expressed physically. This physical embodiment of precepts was a way of participating in a religious community and a way of cultivating oneself. Looking at this list, it is not immediately clear that it forms a basis for martial arts. Still, to the extent that there are Daoist martial arts, I would argue that they are built around similar sets of precepts. The implication is that through the physical practice of these commitments, one gains access to a naturalness or effortlessness which then reveals one's true nature *(zhende)*, one's real potential. Rather merely being than a list of do's and don'ts, Daoist precepts are experiments designed to reveal what it is to be human. These precepts are deep. What does it mean to be honest—truly honest? Can one be honest during sleep? How about while eating? Is it possible to speak truthfully but in an *emotionally* dishonest way? What does one's clothing communicate about honesty? What does it mean to move our bodies in an honest way, say, without vanity or pretense? Is honest movement also simple and efficient? I could go through all nine precepts because I follow them myself, but that would be a different book. I will, however, take a moment to look at the precept, *practice being weak*, because most martial artists recoil at the notion that martial arts have anything to do with cultivating weakness. Yet, most martial arts promise that smaller and weaker practitioners can learn to prevail. Practicing weakness poses the question, just how strong does one need to be? And for what, exactly? This precept isn't advocating being wimpy or sickly; rather, it suggests the use of whole-body mass, leverage, sensitivity, coordination, and efficiency. The precept is not anti-strength; it has a moral basis. In a world where there was rarely enough food, the type of calorie-consuming strength training done these days likely meant that others would go hungry.

Practicing martial arts is like keeping precepts with one's body. When one sinks into a horse stance, what is the goal? What implicit or unconscious contracts are being made? Power for power's sake? Self-control? A look of confidence? A righteous identity? Transcendence of pain and suffering? Long life? Doing well in school? This list could go on and on. It could be darker, too: Taking vengeance? Joining a criminal brotherhood? Remembering our murdered ancestors? Gaining access to the powers of a god? Attaining the strength to survive possession by a demon?

Physical movement, as every actor or dancer knows, can be infused with meaning. The more one practices a particular physicality, and the more intensely one practices it, the stronger the effect of linking commitments or precepts to one's identity becomes.

In modern Chinese martial arts this effect is often referred to in a rather trivial and utilitarian way as *yi*, or intent—generally meaning the embodiment of a specific martial application or technique. But fully conceptualized, it involves re-making one's body—conditioning one's values into the bones. In fact, it was common to say, in a literal fashion, that a sacred text or list of precepts had become so well embodied that it was now "written on one's bones."

Thinking in terms of Daoist precepts, the most potent form of intent is *emptiness*. Rather than getting involved in all the possible values one can attach to a form or to horse stance, why not just make it empty of intent, available? Why not leave it in a potential state—free, uncommitted and unconditioned?

It is this emptiness in movement and stillness which forms the basis of ritual theater, exorcism, Daoist self-cultivation practices, and internal martial arts. Emptiness is the potency which makes each of these traditions effective; at one time they all shared the same cultural milieu. To the actor, emptiness was the prerequisite for becoming someone else on the stage. For the masked amateur performer, being an empty vessel allowed him to become possessed. To the Daoist exorcist, emptiness was a field of power and potency that allowed him to act in chaotic situations without becoming disoriented. To the self-cultivator, emptiness was like a stage, a ritual platform, for visualizing deities in action, or an empty cauldron for brewing *jindan*, the golden elixir of immortality. The Daoist experience of emptiness entails the discarding of rigid identity and conformity; it is unmediated capacity for action—spontaneous, instantaneous, compassionate performance that happens before desire has a chance to arise. To be empty means to have no gap between feeling and action.

An appetite is like an unconscious commitment. Martial arts is something people have a natural appetite for, like sleep, rest, exercise, and food. Humans have appetites for all sorts of things: adventure, cruelty, nurturing, sex, even staring at the wall. Each human shares some of the same appetites, and each human has some unique appetites. The word "appetite" is handy here because it refers to something which fluctuates, sometimes grows in intensity, and sometimes just disappears.

Daoists began to see refining one's appetites as a way of accumulating merit. The idea is that by playing with all the elements of naturally occurring appetites (for food, sleep, exercise, cruelty, fun, stillness, etc.) over time, one can subtly shift them, becoming spontaneously, righteously, and compassionately meritorious. We are our appetites, and our appetites can change. Thus the practice of martial arts can be understood as way to subtly shift our appetites over an extended period of time. This requires active, disciplined experimentation with all our appetites, not just movement and violence, to be effective.

Experimenting with appetites is the basis of what are called hygiene practices, or *macrobiotics*. The way we eat affects the way we feel when we move; the way we sleep affects the clarity of our meditation; the way we socialize affects what sorts of foods we hunger for. Each of these appetites affects the others. If we pay close attention to this process, this mix, over time we can accumulate knowledge about how all these appetites interact. This is a simple form of Daoist alchemy. Daoist alchemy can be complex, drawing in knowledge about the seasons and the stars, exercises, and rare foods that change the way one sees and hears, to create tiny but profound shifts in the felt experience of the body and the environment, but ultimately the fundamental mechanism is the same. Alchemy always involves experimenting with our appetites and paying close attention to the fruition of our conduct. The practice of martial arts fits perfectly into this religious view of what a human being is.

Talismans in the "Land of Rivers and Lakes"

Another way to shed light on martial arts in Chinese religion is to understand how important talismans were. Talismans were everywhere, in everything, integrated into the fabric of life. Martial artists utilized talismans for the obvious things—protection, power, success, and health; but also for achieving enlightenment, speaking the truth, and finding a mate. In this talisman-centric world, even martial skill itself could be understood as a type of talisman.

Writing talismans for healing and protection was a significant activity of early Daoist communities. In one of the world's first examples of a literacy mandate, Daoist initiates were expected to be able to read the *Daodejing* and write talismans. The Chinese word for talisman, *fu*, literally means a "contract." A talisman is a contract between people and the unseen world of gods and ghosts, as well as the unseen world of hopes, dreams, fears, and desires. But talismans were also used for quasi-governmental functions. For instance, a talisman had to be applied to a tree a few days before it was cut. Acquired from a local religious authority, this type of talisman effectively notified people in advance that a claim had been made, and allowed a community to keep track of how many trees were being cut down and where. Marking the tree in advance gave the woodsman time to think about the safest way to cut it down; it also notified the spirits in the tree, and all the animals who lived there, so they would have time to find new homes.

The English word "chop" refers to the stamp that made a talisman official. Word origins are easy to dispute, but dictionaries trace the word "chop" to the Chinese word *kuai*, which means quickly; and "quickly-quickly" is what a Daoist priest says when commanding a visualized assistant to carry off a talisman to the gods.

Talismans often served functions that government permits do today. Before digging clay for pottery, or digging a trench for irrigation, a talisman had to be acquired. Housing construction required talismans before breaking ground, before putting in posts, and to "certify" roof beams. Talismans were ubiquitous.

The spirit world and the material world were not thought of as separate, so naturally they were subject to a single regulatory code; the same regulatory actions covered both. This is pertinent to understanding how martial arts were perceived, how they functioned, and how they were regulated. Talismans are produced by rituals, and they are also the documentation of those rituals. Written manuals, whether for utilitarian or religious purposes, often included talismans or instructions on how to make them. To practice martial arts was, in effect, to ritually make one's body into a talisman of protection.

Practicing martial arts in public was a public statement of intent. Practicing martial arts with the wrong public intent was a crime and a nuisance. Practicing with the "right" intent was an act of public merit. In Chinese, the word for "right" — *zheng*—implies government, healing, and an upright posture. Getting one's students do their stances correctly has layers of embedded historic meaning. The word "public" in Chinese is a homonym with the *gong* in the word *gongfu* (kung fu); they were the same word in an earlier era. *Gong* also refers both to "merit" and a "temple," and by inference, something done in or around a public temple.

As explained in the previous section, precepts, fully embodied, were said to be "written on one's bones." In the same literalist sense, practicing martial arts was understood as a ritual that would turn one's bones into talismans.

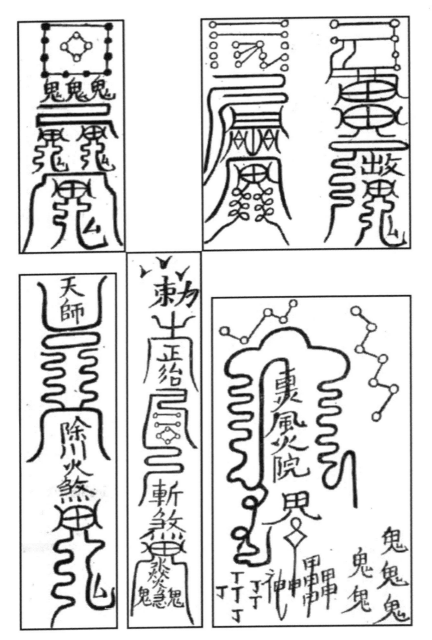

Figure 14. Assorted Talismans, from *The Religious System of China vol. VI*, by J. J. M. de Groot, 1910. Courtesy of The Internet Archive.

Martial arts were practiced in temples both as martial training and theater. The popular epic play, *Outlaws of the Marsh*—inspiration for many kung fu movies—was itself a sacred text, and was treated as a talisman. The Chinese name for this play, *Shuihu*, is literally "water-lake" (also translated as "water-margin"), a synonym with the modern Chinese term *jianghu*, literally "rivers and lakes." What it actually refers to is a land without defined borders, outside of government control, in the shadows; the wilderness; a Chinese "Wild West"; a gangland; a place where people with martial prowess are the spiritual center of the moral order; a place where all problems require martial arts. All kung fu movies take place in the land of *jianghu*. It is a mythic place. But it is also a real place. Anyone engaging in an act of righteous violence who perceives themselves as re-establishing the moral order in a lawless situation, is in the land of *jianghu*. It is a place of extremes. For example, there is more than one play in which the heroine is fighting on a battle field and, in a demonstration of incredible martial prowess, takes a short break to have a baby, before returning to the fight.[22] In this realm, even giving birth could be framed as a heroic form of kung fu. [23]

Outlaws of the Marsh, like many similar collections of entertaining plays, was a religious ritual that displayed martial skills. The imagined set for this type of play was the *jianghu*, and martial-arts training was the symbolic talisman one needed to enter the *jianghu*.

Perhaps we are inclined to think of rivers and roads as public freeways, but in historic China, besides the constant threat of bandits and other unpleasant people who lived along the way and wouldn't hesitate to take one's belongings—there was a general notion that one should have a good reason to be on the road. The convention was that a person needed to carry a note, a tally, explaining the purpose of his journey. These needed to be stamped by a village head, a magistrate, or a spiritual leader (like the abbot of a monastery), or bear an imperial seal. These documents let people know that a traveler had a reason for being on the road, that she wasn't a bandit, and also clarified whether it was appropriate to seek a nominal sum for safe passage. They also let violent people know that if something bad happened to the bearer, others would come seeking retribution.

---

22   Roland Altenburger, *The Sword or the Needle: the Female Knight-Errant (Xia) in Traditional Chinese Narrative*. Vol. 15. Peter Lang, 2009.
23   Giving birth on the stage (to a fake baby) was a popular scene in the Chinese opera of California during the gold rush era, see Daphne P. Lei, *Operatic China*, p. 59-60.

These documents were in effect a type of talisman; in fact, historically it might have been the other way around: these travel documents may have been the original model for written talismans. The "spiritual version" of these travel documents was issued in order to protect the holder against assault by ghosts and demons. In effect, talismans granted the holder permission to conduct difficult business is a world inhabited by chaotic and dangerous unseen forces.

Some talisman were curses used for malevolent intent, somewhat like the "evil eye" was used everywhere from Europe to India. But even talismanic curses were conceptualized as "warrants"— written documents giving a person permission to kill, torture, and capture enemies.

In the popular imagination, the "land of rivers and lakes" was firstly any place outside of one's home village, outside of the known. And secondly, it was any place outside the direct authority of the emperor. The land of rivers and lakes was an accessible mythic space; it could really be anywhere one could hide or disappear to. Monasteries in the mountains, like the Chan Buddhist Shaolin Temple, or the Daoist Wudang Mountain, were part of the land of rivers and lakes in the popular imagination—they where places where the actions of men of prowess determined right and wrong. This idea has been heavily developed in fiction, theater, and film.

Before a Daoist hermit journeyed into a mountain wilderness, she would generally make complex astro-calendarical calculations to determine the best time and place for travel; she would then use these calculations to make talismans and attach them to her clothing. Bronze mirrors are an ancient form of these talismans. Perhaps taking a dig at Daoist vanity, Buddhist nuns were known to claim that a perfectly empty mind was the only talisman (mirror) they needed to enter the wilderness.

Brotherhoods, Theater History, and the Gods

Theatricality has always been embedded in religion, and martial arts have been a part of that as far back in history as we can see.

Sworn brotherhoods, both within Chinese society and around its margins, have been a source of religious identity bolstered by martial prowess and infused with theatricality. Founded on a commitment to mutual aid, these sworn oaths were key units of Chinese religious and social organization.

Figure 15. Silver Backed Bronze Mirror (backside is polished smooth), ~700 CE. Photographed 1909, TO-EI-SHU-KO, 1st edition, 5th vol. Tokyo, Japan, published by Shinbi-Shoin. Courtesy of Wikimedia.

In his unpublished 1983 thesis in anthropology, *Marginality and the Hero's Art*, Daniel Amos investigated a practice in Hong Kong called *shenda* ("spirit hitting") and its relationship to secret societies. Amos's work deals with the performative aspects of brotherhoods and how closely they are associated with criminality. A portion of his research was done in post–Cultural Revolution China, and it is astounding how many people he found in secret martial arts groups. Pointing to the theatrical nature of claiming the secret status of a knight errant *(wuxia)* from the land of rivers and lakes *(jianghu)*, Amos suggested that martial arts were widely use as a muted form of social protest. His informant's identities were built around *wuxia* literature—they were not just familiar with it; they brought it to life as ritually bonded sworn brothers. A parallel identity in politically freer Hong Kong could open up an entire way of life, whether as a martial arts teacher, a gangster, or a film actor.

Secret societies generally have mysterious beginnings. In China they developed as rebel organizations with a mutual aid component, and recruited heavily among the lower castes of society—the toughest of the tough—but they also sought recruits from within the civil administration and disaffected gentry. They used elaborate initiation rituals, secret codes and handshakes, and organizational structures that prioritized prowess over birth.

In the 1980s, the Hong Kong police claimed that the majority of martial-arts schools had links to the major secret society called the Tiandihui—better known in English as the Triads. Amos parses this claim with data showing that at any given martial-arts school actual involvement in the Triads varied, ranging from almost none, or perhaps one student who used to be a member when he was young, to membership actually being a requirement for entrance into the school.

Shenda (spirit hitting) is a broad category of transgressive religious martial-arts practices that confer protective powers, fighting prowess, and invoke the realm of spirits. They are generally part of secret sworn brotherhoods, so Amos had a hard time estimating how widespread they were, yet he managed to attend several different types of *shenda* rituals and report on them. He suggests that the martial skills learned in these "cults" are pathways to entrance and promotion within the secret societies, especially at the lower ends of those hierarchies. *Shenda* practitioners also used their connection to the gods for healing, sorcery, and fortune-telling.

Amos described an initiation which has parallels with the practices of the Boxer rebels (1898–1900). It involved developing extraordinary powers through devotion to a martial deity on a special *shenda* altar. After following specific ritual protocols, the initiated sworn brother was chopped across the stomach with a large machete-like knife. If the initiate was sincere, Amos was told, the god would welcome him and the wound would not bleed. Other extraordinary powers related to fighting were expected to come over time with devotion to the cult.

Another type of ritual Amos attended involved young men, sworn brothers, going into a type of trance in which they became a popular martial god—often the gods of opera, like the monkey king Sun Wukong, his friend Piggy, or Guan Gong, the god of war. The youths in these rituals would often fight each other as the gods, staying in character and in the trance state. This type of sparring was seen as preparation for real-life violence. Generally, proof of true possession by a god was demonstrated by the inability to remember anything that had happened while possessed. Sometimes one god would teach another god's martial-arts routines, which were apparently invented on the spot; improvisation was used as a vehicle for transcending the constraints of normal identity and social inhibitions. These spontaneous plays could include ghosts, demons, and a wide variety of gods and immortals. Other cult members or outsider guests like Amos could interact with the deities without themselves becoming possessed; Amos was allowed to ask questions of the gods. Interestingly, a distinction was made between cult members who could go into trances easily (they had the ability to call their deity to them) and those who had to act out ritual sublimation first before becoming possessed.

Shenda-type rituals must have been widely practiced. One of the cults Amos features claimed twenty-four previous masters, which, although unlikely, would date the cult back to the Ming Dynasty (1368–1644). The rituals Amos witnessed were taking place in the southern part of China in the 1980s, but the similarities to the ritual practices of the northern Boxer rebels are unmistakable. The possessing deities are taken from the same list of opera characters.

The whole idea of possession, of acting outside of one's identity without taking responsibility for it, and even claiming to not remember, is profoundly outside of the Western cultural framework. I imagine, however, that seasoned criminals in America are so used to lying about their activities that it would be a useful trick of the mind for them to think of the criminal self as being someone else. This is an important issue, because antisocial behavior often requires the criminal to identify his victim as an "other," or as somehow deserving of the crime. Before harming someone, most people have to convince themselves that the person they are striking is evil, racist, or degenerate. This dehumanizing process may function in reverse within these particular Chinese subcultures; that is, to harm someone as a god is to super-humanize oneself, rather than to dehumanize the "other."

Amos may have been the first, if not the only person to gain entrance to mainland China's martial-arts communities as a researcher in the years immediately after the horrors of the Cultural Revolution. He discovered an active semi-secret society of martial artists at the local level. They were mostly trying to avoid being noticed, but in contrast to the defanged government-sponsored Wushu organizations, they gathered to train real fighting skills. Amos also discovered a deep longing for martial arts in the youth, who were using them as a kind of theater of dream—a place to put aside the hopelessness of the present and actually become an individual; a place to fantasize about becoming great and to develop a sense of self-worth.

Avron Boretz made similar observations in his book—as can be seen from its title—*Gods, Ghosts, and Gangsters: Ritual Violence, Martial Arts, and Masculinity on the Margins of Chinese Society.*[24] Boretz explores the contemporary subculture of truck drivers in southwestern China and how they identify as part of an alternate moral universe called the "land of rivers and lakes" *(jianghu)*, a theatrically inspired land beyond the the control of civilization, where men of prowess establish their own morality with grit and guile, righteousness and reciprocity. Earlier we discussed Boretz's explorations of the *songjiang* troops, the demon generals who accompany martial gods from the temple to the stage. These troops were sworn brotherhoods. In fact, *songjiang* troops derive their name from the lead bandit character Wu Song of *Outlaws of the Marsh*—which is sometimes rendered in English as *All Men Are Brothers.* Wu Song and his fellow bandits are the model of sworn brotherhoods, as are Guan Gong and his sworn brothers from the epic *Three Kingdoms.*

Conclusion

Chinese religions are built around three key organizational conceptual practices: precepts, talismans, and sworn oaths. Martial-arts movement and practice are so deeply integrated with all three that, historically and

---

24   Avron Boretz, *Gods, Ghosts, and Gangsters: Ritual Violence, Martial Arts, and Masculinity on the Margins of Chinese Society.* University of Hawai'i Press, 2015.

culturally speaking, martial arts were in fact martial religion. Seen from the point of view of Chinese religion, martial arts are simply one way of expressing the commitments of a religious life.

More Ways Religion Defines Martial Arts

In the previous section we explained the three basic components of Chinese religion: precepts, talismans, and sworn oaths. In this chapter we will examine the two primary themes of Chinese religions—the power of *yin*, and exorcisms—showing how they are expressed in martial theater, martial skills, and warfare. Again, we will demonstrate that historically they were part of a single worldview, a unified way of acting and being in the world.

The Power of Yin

In Chinese religious cosmology, martial arts are *yin*. Women are the *yin* gender, and *yin* is a type of power associated with chaos, death, urine, blood, sex, and darkness. Martial artists sometimes think of martial arts as male and therefore *yang*, but this is a serious failure to understand the subject in context. Martial arts are *yin* because they are associated with blood and death. This subject deserves a closer look.

Chinese tradition did not make strong distinctions between history, fiction, and religion the way modern societies do. Ritual-theater traditions were the main source of historical knowledge for traditional villagers, and woman warriors were well represented on the stage as drivers of martial culture, even though they did not serve in government armies. Professional theater was associated with sex and prostitution; thus, it was also *yin*. In ritual theater, ghosts and demons were the most *yin* things; the entrance to a stage itself, the stage-door, was called the ghost-gate *(guimen)*, because, from a religious point of view, everything represented on the stage—heroes, ghosts, spirits, gods, ancestors—was dead.

Feminine religious power is found in many aspects of martial arts and martial theater. In martial plays, *yin* defeated *yang*. When female characters won, it was because of their *yin* magic. When male characters won it was because they used some form of *yin* power. Pure *yang* heroes did indeed sometimes triumph in martial plays; conformity to the orthodoxy of the Confucian state demanded it, but they did so by enlisting female or demonic forces. Great male martial heroes of the theater inevitably attempted to contain or control *yin*, and their *yang* maleness was never sufficient to accomplish this task. It is a running joke in Chinese opera that *yin* becomes *yang* and *yang* becomes *yin*—after all, Chinese opera developed with either all-male or all-female troupes, and before the twentieth century half the character roles battling on the stage were cross-dressing.

In the popular imagination bandits, rebels, and religious cults were often indistinguishable. Women were welcome in the bandit-rebel-cult realm of rivers and lakes *(jianghu)*, where accounts of women in powerful positions were symbols of potency. Prominent women of the *jianghu* often came from performing families, especially before the 1700s, when women were officially banned from performing—a change that likely inspired some female performers to join rebellions. Powerful women represented both real and symbolic opposition to the dominant Confucian state. Naturally, the theatrical realm reflected this. (See *Opera as Rebellion* sub-chapter.) Warrior women had magical powers in nearly every play. Real-life women in the world of bandit-rebel cults were thought to have comparable magic powers. Male bandit-rebel cult leaders often married female religious masters of magic, acrobatics, and martial arts, as detailed below.

These ideas about *yin* power were prevalent in warfare. Women's blood, urine, and nakedness were used tactically to pollute the enemy's *yang* purity, making them impotent, or to overwhelm the enemy's *yin* powers with stronger *yin* powers. Women warriors who took the field were inspirational martial religious leaders. (As an aside, these "women" may not have been biological women—since gender is performative, we have no way of knowing.) Fan Pen Li Chen's book, *Chinese Shadow Theatre, History, Popular Religion, and Women Warriors*, is an excellent resource for history, fables, and legends of women in warfare:

Very few women warriors have actually been recorded by Chinese historians. Considering the amount of historical data in existence and the amount of information on male warriors, one can only conclude that very few women served in the orthodox Chinese armies. There are indications, however, that many women warriors existed in foreign tribes, in barbarian states, in bandit strongholds, in independent stockades, and among rebels, especially among religious rebel armies. Since Chinese historians were inherently prejudiced against these groups, the few such women recorded in the Chinese histories likely represent the tip of the iceberg. Their images in popular novels, military romances, and shadow plays represent the glorification and mythification of such characters by commoners who readily accepted the existence of women warriors and who revered their superhuman and supernatural powers and were sympathetic to their activities and causes.[25]

Chen discusses dozens of important female warriors, such as the iconic female sword master who taught the troops for king Gojian, the source of the ubiquitous Chinese saying "eat bitter" (chiku)—a story as well known in north Asia as Cinderella is in the west. Then there was Empress Ma (1338–82), the warrior daughter of rebel leaders who helped her husband found the Ming dynasty. Miss Cai led Muslim rebel cavalries during the Nian Rebellion in the 1800s. Countless pirate leaders were women; Zheng I Sao, a former prostitute who became known as the Dragon Lady of the South China Sea, is the most famous. Several women are lauded in tales of the eighteenth-century White Lotus rebellions, including five female generals and Woman He, whose throwing knives could kill a man from a hundred feet on horseback at full gallop. Qiu Ersao (1822–53) was a leader of a Heaven-Earth Society (Tiandihui), as was Su Sanniang; they were both known for their martial prowess. Two female leaders of the Taiping rebellion (1851–1865) were bandit chiefs before they joined the rebellion; and Hong Zuanjiao, the wife of the Taiping Western King, was known for her awesome sword skills in battle. The Eight Trigrams Uprising (Baguajiao, 1821–51) boasted an entire female army: "Generals Cheng Sijie and Yang Wujie...wove among enemy forces in the style of 'butterflies flitting among flowers,' wielding broadswords on horseback, their hairpins glittering in the light."[26]

---

25   Fan Ben Li Chen, *Chinese Shadow Theatre, History, Popular Religion, and Women Warriors* (Montreal: McGill-Queen's University Press, 2007), 117.
26   Chen, *Chinese Shadow*, p.121-123

Figure 16. Woman Warrior from Beijing Opera (gender?), ~1905. Image courtesy of Penelope Fowler and Historical Photographs of China, University of Bristol.

Knowing the individual stories of women warriors is fun, but it is less important than understanding that in the popular imagination, women represented the necessity of *yin* power. For example, "Wang Lun, who rebelled in 1774 in Shandong, had an "adopted daughter" in name, mistress in fact, by the name of Wu Sanniang; she was one of Wang's most powerful warriors. Originally an itinerant performer highly skilled in boxing, tightrope walking, and acrobatics, she terrified the enemy with spellbinding magic. She brought a dozen associates from her old life to the sect, and they all became fearsome warriors known as 'female immortals.'" "...A tall, white-haired woman at least sixty years old, possibly the mother of one of three acrobat-turned-women-warriors, wielded one sword with ease and two almost as effortlessly. Dressed in yellow astride a horse, hair loose and flying, she was feared as much for her sorcery as for her military skills. Her presence indicates that some of the women came from female-dominated itinerant performing families."[27]

China has a long history of military strategist stretching back to Sunzi's *Art of War,* which can seem quite modern in its strong preference for systematic strategies and tactics that win wars. But the practical reality of everyday violence in China was imbued with mystical forces, including the tactical use of magical blood and urine invariably gathered from women.

The amount of mystical power attributed to success and failure in violent encounters—whether small, intimate affairs or massive battles—cannot be overstated. Incantations, talismans and talismanic substances, medicines, deity invocation and possession, spells, rituals of purification and empowerment, masks, garments, animal totems, and magical implements were used to increase one's power. This was the case in every aspect of preparation for violence, from the makers of swords and armor, who imbued them with magical substances, to the generals performing obligatory divination rituals before battle. People sharpened their swords, but they also tied them with amulets, gave them spiritually potent names, and dedicated them in rituals.

Likewise, every effort was made to damage an enemy or mitigate a threat. Both divine and demonic forces were enlisted to harm, hamper, or overcome adversaries. Spiritual pollution was utilized to disempower opposing forces, and was often blamed as the cause of failure. The power of women's menstrual blood was understood to be a particularly powerful pollutant, as were the urine and naked bodies of women, which were used tactically to defeat enemies on the battlefield.

---

27   Chen, *Chinese Shadow,* p.121-123.

For example, during the Boxer Rebellion (Yihequan, 1898–1900), ideas that connected religious devotion, theatrical characters, magic, and martial arts were not only widely held, but were the stuff of daily life. The Boxers claimed to be invulnerable to bullets, improving on a long history of martial conditioning regimes which claimed to make people invulnerable to steel-edged weapons.

> The Boxers regularly attributed the casualties they suffered in fighting with foreigners in Tianjin to the latter's placement of naked women in the midst or in front of their forces, which broke the power of the Boxers' magic. A story circulated and widely believed by the populace was that a naked woman had straddled each of the many cannons mounted in the foreign buildings in Zizhulin, making it impossible for the "gunfire-repelling magic" *(bipao zhifa)* of the Boxers to work properly.[28]

> Dirty water, as a destroyer of magic, was unquestionably related in Boxer minds to the most powerful magic-inhibitor of all: women, and more particularly uncleanness in women—a category that, for the Boxers, included everything from menstrual or fetal blood to nakedness to pubic hair. Water, of course, was a symbol of *yin*, the primeval female principle in China, and there was a long-held belief that the symbolic representation of *yin* could be used to overcome the effects of phenomena symbolic of the male principle, *yang*, such as fire and gunfire. Several groups of rebels in the late Ming dynasty used women to suppress the firepower of government troops. During the insurgency of 1774 in Shandong, Wang Lun's forces used an array of magical techniques, including strange incantations and women soldiers waving white fans, in their assault on Linqing. The imperial defenders of the city were at first frustrated by the effectiveness of the rebels' fighting tactics. An old soldier, however, came to the rescue with this advice: "Let a prostitute go up on the wall and take off her underclothing…we will use yin power to counter their spells." When this proposal was carried out and proved effective, the government side

---

28   Paul A. Cohen. *History in Three Keys: The Boxers as Event, Experience, and Myth.* Columbia University Press, 1997. p.131

adopted additional measures of a like sort, including (as later recounted by Wang Lun himself) "women wearing red clothing but naked from the waist down, bleeding and urinating in order to destroy our power."[29]

Chinese Words

Chinese words normally consist of two characters joined together; however, some of the key terms describing Chinese cosmology are single characters. Single characters are often polysemous: they have many meanings. For example, the term *jingshen*, which means "attention," is most often used in the negative, as in *meiyou jingshen*, "You aren't paying attention." But *jing* and *shen* by themselves are key cosmological terms. The term *jing* can mean sperm, essence, self-reproducing, pure form, or the non-animated aspect of a living body (i.e., just the bag of flesh). The term *shen* can mean god(s), spirit, spatial perception, imagination, and mental acuity. The context of these polysemous terms is essential to understanding them. There is hardly any term more polysemous than *qi*, which is usually made more obscure by attempts at translation. The polysemous nature of these terms means that they are sometimes stretched and distorted to fit arguments; however, the terms *jing*, *qi*, and *shen* together represent a very specific cosmology. *Qi* can simply mean "presence" in the theater. *Qi* is not a *yin* or a *yang* substance—although in a medical context, for example, *qi* is considered *yang* relative to blood, which is very *yin*. Likewise, *qi* is often represented in art by spiraling clouds; the sky is *yang*, the fluffy white part is *yang*, and the moisture is *yin*. All things are in a state of continuous change, and are therefore both *yin* and *yang*. Although challenging at first, grasping the way polysemous language is used will make Chinese cosmology easier to understand without sacrificing its intentional ambiguity.

Internal and External Defined

All of this has direct bearing on how martial arts were understood. Fully conceived, martial arts were a way of using *yin* to fight *yin*. Demonic *yin* is polluting, and has to be mitigated or cleaned out. Yet *yin* is what ultimately will damage the enemy, so it must be cultivated with great care. There are two basic approaches, internal and external.

The difference between internal and external martial arts is hard to understand, especially in translation, but being a native speaker

---

29   Cohen 1997: 129-130

of Chinese is itself not a great advantage either because the basic cosmology has been obscured by modernity. The following may require more than one reading.

To grasp the distinction between internal and external, we must look at two conceptual frameworks at the same time: *yin-yang*, and *jing-qi-shen*. *Yin* and *yang* are always relative. To say that darkness is yin and brightness is *yang* is true, but it is only relatively true; a dark object can still be yang relative to an object which is more *yin*. *Jing, qi*, and *shen* always exist together, but they can be distinct from each other or mix together. In the practice of internal martial arts, the physical body is *yin* and *jing*. It is the non-animated aspect of a living body—the flesh and bones. *Yang* is outside the body; it is called *shen*, often translated "spirit," and refers to spatial perception, both felt and imagined. *Qi* is the intermediary between these two; it is neither yin nor yang. In this cosmology, qi is what makes things unique, because it holds things together in a form or a shape for a period of time. Without *qi*, *shen* would float away, and *jing* would be absorbed by the earth. When the physical body is completely empty *(xu)* of intent, *qi* floats off like clouds surrounding the body. The *yang* spirit then leads the *yin* body without touching it directly; thus *yang* (spirit) avoids becoming polluted by *yin* (flesh). *Qi* functions as the intermediary between *yin* and *yang*. Thus, in this classic reversal, a completely empty body *(yin)* is led by the spirit[30] *(yang)*—but only the *yin* part, the empty body, the weapon, makes physical contact with the enemy.

"Internal" thus refers to a specific order of action.

There are variants of this; for instance, in Daoist ritual empty spaces felt within the body can be visualized as *palaces*, which become homes for powerful deities—but the basic cosmology holds: those palaces have to be empty before the deities can be activated in them.

Some internal martial artists may be hearing this for the first time, despite having practiced for many years. Because the cosmology is so often presented in an ambiguous way, most internal martial artists are actually practicing a mix of internal and external methods. But the same holds for most external martial artists: they are mostly practicing a mixed method.

---

30   Spirits—what in the West are called non-corporeal spirits—are considered dead, and therefore *yin*, in China. But actually, in Chinese cosmology they are tied to the living via a bit of something solid (called *ling*), like hair, a bone, an object of devotion like a piece of clothing imbued with bodily fluids, or even a strong lingering emotion in a living person. So in Chinese cosmology, ghosts are corporeal, but just a little bit.

Figure 17. Qi Clouds around the deity Cai Yun, from Ping Sien Si, Perak, Malaysia, 2014. Photo: Ananjoti (Photo Dharma), Creative Commons, courtesy of Wikimedia.

In the practice of external martial arts, the integrity of the physical body is protected by infusing it with *qi*. Martial intent *(yi)* is used to drive spirit *(shen)*—the spatial imagination—into the flesh and bones, so that the body becomes more *yang*—tough, solid, and impenetrable. When the spirit *(shen)* is violently forced out, either in ritual preparations for battle (using talismans and theatricality—both *yin*), or in the event of a surprise attack (also *yin*), the body becomes suddenly vacant *(xu)*. The vacant body is then aided, or sometimes completely possessed, by ghost-spirits *(guishen)*, who do the actual fighting. *Guishen* use the physical *yin* body as a weapon—a weapon that has been forged through training which gradually infused it with *yang* intent.

When modern martial-arts practitioners hear about the *yin* origins of martial arts, they sometimes react with shock and disbelief. But consider that the adrenalized state itself was viewed as a kind of possession by *yin* spirits, or gods. The adrenalized state is associated with numbness, loss of fine motor control, freezing, panic, altered perceptions, difficulty making decisions, and even blacking out. It is an accessible experience, and not so far out of the ordinary. Traditional cosmology was a creative and practical explanation of something real. In the modern world people do not hesitate to say that someone is "haunted" by their experiences on the battlefield. Whether we believe in ghosts is beside the point; the idea of haunting continues to have resonance.

Because most schools of Chinese martial arts are cut off from the religious origins of the arts, they are also cut off from accurate historical explanations of the cosmology that created the arts. Recovering the original cosmology opens up new insights into the arts.

The Santeria martial-dance rituals of Afro-Cuba offer a meaningful comparison. In Santeria, both the drummers and the priests are forbidden to become possessed by the gods, whereas initiates do become possessed. From an observer's point of view, a priest or priestess appears to be doing the exact same ritual dances—which embody the character attributes of the gods—as the initiates are. Yet one can be possessed by the god and the other cannot.

Similar cosmologies guide Chinese martial arts. The exact same distinction between possessed (external), and not-possessed (internal) is used in Daoist rituals. The secret inner parts of the rituals done by higher Daoist priests *(daoshi gaogong)* do not involve possession; the outer parts, performed publicly by other sorts of ritual experts and mediums, do involve becoming possessed by the gods.

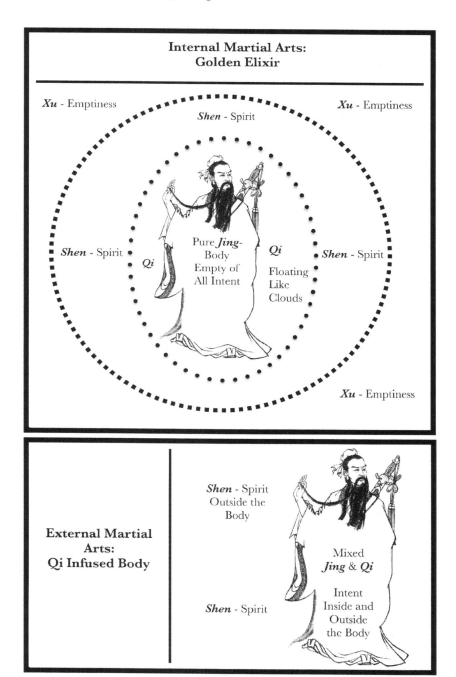

Figure 18. Internal vs. external diagram.

Theatrical performance also has two categories in practice, masked trance-possession by deities, and skilled performance of the deities.

An individual Chinese martial-arts style can be practiced either as an external art or an internal one. Both types of cosmology-in-action are accessible through martial movement.

Modern people are often embarrassed by religion, so it's not surprising that the religious origins of martial arts became hidden. Everyone's ancestors did great and terrible things—that is the human condition. We are tragic beings. But covering up history is worse than being embarrassed by it because it creates confusion for the next generation. Sadly, the last few generations of Chinese martial artists and Chinese theater professionals were often beaten for asking such questions of their teachers.

I don't claim to really understand deity possession cults. To me, they seem like a form of improvisational theater created by people who were often on the edge of starvation. Yet, considering that these possession traditions are spread so widely across the globe, it is worth investigating what insights can be gleaned from them. Keith Johnstone, author of *Impro, Improvisation for the Theatre*, says that good masked performance is a form of trance-possession; when a mask "turns on," the entity that performs is much the same regardless of who is wearing it. He describes the improvisational state as the absence of the voices in our heads, a kind of vacancy. People are often afraid of improving because it requires giving up control. And yet, a martial-arts tradition without the capacity to improvise is like a sacred mask in a museum, an object of beauty separated from context and meaning.

Conclusion

The distinction between internal and external martial arts is difficult to understand because of the distance modern people have from the religious context that first articulated it. It is often assumed that external martial arts already existed and then someone came along and invented internal martial arts. While possibly correct, that assumption contributes to the confusion because it skirts the issue of how external martial arts were perceived historically.

In China, the most common forms of martial arts invoked the gods, either through taking on the physicality of a martial theatrical-role, or through enlisting the gods to fight alongside, or possess, the artist's body.

Daoist alchemy had a huge impact on martial arts. External alchemy is mixing and drinking herbs and drugs that transform one into an immortal. It is call *waidan*, literally external elixir. Internal alchemy, *neidan*, turns the practitioner into an immortal through meditation and visualization. In the ritual version of *neidan*, one visualizes the gods outside of one's body, and controls them like puppets. The Daoist ritual master is thus considered a kind of puppet master of the gods.

Plays in which a character practices inner alchemy and thus achieves superior martial prowess were common in the Ming Dynasty, certainly by 1500. The idea that the practice of inner alchemy confers martial prowess is probably at least two hundred years older. As will become clear in the next section, the reason inner alchemy is associated with martial prowess is that it was conceptualized as a powerful form of exorcism. The notion that external martial arts are a purely physical practice is modern. By contrast, internal martial arts are much older. However, if the term 'external martial arts' is referring to an even older tradition, then it is one thoroughly entwined with religious culture.

Exorcism as a Central Organizing Principle

The urgent need to be protected from *yin*, the demonic and feminine forces all around us, is the reason exorcism is such a primary theme and practice in Chinese traditional culture. The ways in which ideas about exorcism define Chinese martial arts are not at all obvious at first glance.

Though the concept of exorcism often triggers strong reactions in modern people, responses vary. My own mother read the book *The Exorcist*—before it was a movie—and thought the whole thing was a hysterical comedy. It wasn't until the film came out that it occurred to her that some people might find it frightening.

All traditional Chinese theater was ritual, and most of it had exorcistic functions. This is not nearly as foreign to our modern experience as one might think. The two biggest genres of plays written for traditional Chinese opera, to put a modern spin on it, were "chick flicks" with kung fu (called *qing*, or passion plays), and horror films with kung fu— basically ghost stories and hellish adventures. When I'm feeling down, I like to go see a horror film because it reminds me that my life really isn't that bad—hey, at least my neighbors aren't chainsaw-wielding maniacs. My wife on the other hand, likes chick flicks. They make her laugh, though I have no idea why. If she forces me to go with her, I end up (this is top secret information) in a puddle of tears. Why she laughs at people being mean to each other I will never understand. But she hates

Figure 19. People attending an Opera Outdoors. Est. 1907-1915, Shanxi? Image courtesy of Lydia Parbury and Historical Photographs of China, University of Bristol.

horror movies, so there. The cathartic experiences we both have with these genres of film are in a small way exorcistic. We use the experience of going to the movies to clear out fears and anxieties, stagnant feelings, *yin*. Exorcisms in China were an experience of a different order and scale than going to a movie, but the operative mechanisms are part of a common core of human experiences. Operas were just one form of ritual exorcism.

What are the elements of exorcism?

Exorcism includes the following elements: purification, sacrificial offerings, creating divine images, emptiness as a source of potency, and cosmic rectification.

Purification is a form of cleaning that includes bathing, simple meditation, sweeping, washing, and fasting. The goal is to clear away what is dead or lingering *(yin)*. Another type of purification is more aggressive: firecrackers, stamping the ground, loud gongs, and shouting, to frighten away yin spirits. Martial arts incorporate both types of purification: we practice to clear away poor movement habits, and we practice with vigor to display prowess.

Sacrificial offerings involve shedding blood, either real or symbolic. This part of exorcism is truly ancient. Originally it involved human sacrifice, the old way of dealing with conquered warriors and their family members. The large rivers in China took many lives during floods, so a tradition developed of offering human sacrifices in hope of appeasing the gods. Gradually, sacrifices shifted to animals, becoming successively less onerous: elephants, then oxen, sheep, dogs, chickens, and finally insects. Large amounts of grain sometimes replaced animal sacrifice; this then became alcohol, which is the concentrated essence *(jing)* of grain. Yet by definition, Daoist exorcism does not offer blood sacrifice, since Daoist offerings must be non-aggressive *(wuwei)*. Instead, they offer paper animals to be burned, symbolic amounts of grain, talismans written in red cinnabar ink (the color of blood), drawings, incense, water infused with the ashes of burnt paper talismans, flowers, sword dances, plays, and martial-arts performances.

Divine images can be created through visualization, a dedicated statue, a painting or other symbolic object, a masked performance, or the presentation of a theatrical character. Divine images are manifestations of the imagination infused with power; in the Shamanic framing of exorcism they overwhelm or kill, in the Daoist framing they return, rectify or resolve all aggression and conflicting emotions back to Dao—unnamable, not-knowing, emptiness.

Emptiness is a central metaphor of East Asian cosmology. There are many types of emptiness; that of a container, that of a puppet, that of a stage; being without intention, desire, or meaning—vacuous, without form, and limitless. Exorcisms begin and end with the invocation of emptiness.

The goal of all exorcism in China is some form of cosmic rectification. The ritual function of operas and other exorcisms was, in a broad sense, to create alliances in both the human and the unseen supernatural worlds. The goals of those alliances were protection, harmony, and the sharing of resources. In the unseen realm of gods and demons, the ritual aspects of exorcism were intended to protect against chaotic forces like unchecked violence, diseases, and natural disasters (yin). Regular exorcisms maintained dynamic and reciprocal relationships with local gods, spirits, and ancestors; and between families and villages in a given region. An opera, like all exorcisms, was a form of contract between the spirit world (the dead) and human constituencies (the living).

Meditation can be conceptualized as an exorcism, as can taking precepts, making talismans, or swearing oaths. Buddhism, Daoism, Confucianism, and local cults all defined their purposes and values with exorcism as a common theme. As I will show, martial arts were also understood as a form of exorcism.

Confucianism is founded on the idea that one inherits a great deal from their ancestors, including body, culture, and circumstances. To some extent, one also inherits will, intentions, and goals. The Confucian worldview is predicated on the idea that one has a duty to carry out and comprehend one's ancestors' intentions in a way which is compatible with one's own circumstances and experiences. In practice, it is entirely possible to have two ancestors who died with conflicting goals, or an ancestor who died with an unfulfilled desire, like unrequited love; or—one of Confucius's favorite discussions—a parent who plotted to kill us. Dead ancestors are like spirits whose intentions linger on in one's habits and reactions to stress. The central purpose of Confucianism is to resolve these conflicts and lingering feelings of distress through a continuous process of self-reflection and upright conduct. Ultimately, the goal is to leave a better world for one's descendants, with open-ended possibilities, support, and clarity of purpose. This is summarized in the terms harmony (he), rectification (zheng), and unity (yi).

The Confucian purpose is fundamentally built on the metaphor of an exorcism. Clear aside one's own agenda and contemplate the full intentions (i.e., offerings) of one's ancestors, visualize them in a material way (i.e., imagine), reflect them into emptiness so that they can be understood relative to current circumstances, then take that refined understanding and transform it into action. Clear, offer, imagine, empty, repair—this is what Confucius meant when he said that we should strive to make all of our actions ritually correct *(li)*.

Martial-arts forms are inheritances from the ancestors of a particular lineage; an exact way of practicing, not a way of thinking. They have no absolute explanation of purpose; that is what must be discovered through daily practice, daily ritual.

Practicing a particular form is a process of reanimating the movement of the ancestors who created it. Learning a form is a process of uncovering and integrating the movement insights of all the ancestors in a given lineage. Implicitly hidden in the movement is a composite of how each of those ancestors felt about themselves and the world.

This process of reanimating a form can further be understood as correcting the errors embedded in the form as it was inherited—in a sense, healing the ancestors. Practicing a form can also be conceptualized as healing one's parents or one's genetic ancestors, because the way we move is already an embodiment of the way our ancestors moved. In this paradigm, *gongfu* (martial skill) acquired through reanimating a form is a way of perfecting one's body. Since our flaws are either inherited through our parents or acquired via our own bad habits, the practice of a form becomes a conduct correcting process. *Gongfu* is a kind of efficacy; it rectifies the inappropriate, aggressive, and wasteful movement and breathing habits that we learned from our ancestors or acquired through bad conduct. —Clear, offer, imagine, empty, rectify.

Martial-arts practice is a daily personal exorcism, a sweeping away of the lingering influences of the unresolved dead. This goes a long way toward explaining why, for instance, itinerant monks or priests soliciting money would perform martial-arts routines for the public—they were demonstrating the merit they had accumulated (and shared) through this self-correcting process.

The same mechanism also worked in reverse, using fear. Members of the professional beggar caste were feared because they were seen as negative omens. They had their own styles of martial arts.[31] Beggars

---

31   See Leung Ting's *Skills of the Vagabonds*, Leung Ting Company, Hong Kong (1986).

threatened to crash weddings and other important events if they were not paid off—which they invariably were. Public solicitors and performers wielded forms of magical influence thought to be accumulated through either positive merit or anti-merit. The potential dark side of martial arts is never far away; it is only mitigated by righteous conduct—that is, commitment to future generations.

A common criticism of Chinese martial-arts forms is that they are "empty" in the pejorative sense of being meaningless and useless. But the forms should be empty. This criticism is the result of a disconnect between the origins of the arts and their contemporary practice. Lacking a conceptual grounding in the history of exorcistic practice, most schools make an effort to enhance the forms by teaching applications for each movement. Applications are demonstrations of how a conflict might transpire. In practice, however, applications tend to fail, and the reason they fail is lack of *gongfu*. *Gongfu* is a quality of movement which has efficacy regardless of the techniques employed. If a person has *gongfu*, they have it when they are taking out the trash or setting the table. They have it on the stage, during ritual, in times of stress, and in times of calm.

Loss of conceptual continuity between past and contemporary practice has led to many aspects of the arts being discarded. Exorcism is just one example of this. Fortunately, since these are classical arts, a great deal of material has simply been passed on without explanation. Once the actual historical milieu from which the arts were born is understood, the arts can be recontextualized and re-imagined. Even the process of discarding can be deeply creative and inspiring, especially when it is grounded in historically and culturally coherent knowledge.

Martial Theater as Exorcism

Nuo, or dance exorcisms, as described in Jo Riley's book *Chinese Theatre and The Actor in Performance*,[32] begin with a ritual emptying of spirits from the performers' bodies. These spirits, called the three *hun* and seven *po*, making ten altogether, polarize in our bodies and disperse at death: the *hun* go up, and the *po* go down. Before *nuo* performances, extractive talismans are used to remove the *hun* and *po*, which are then stored in vessels for safe keeping. Amateur performers then don masks triggering

---

32   Jo Riley, *Chinese Theatre and the Actor in Performance*. Vol. 3. Cambridge University Press, 1997.

deity possession without fear of harm. After performing the exorcism, which is a type of play, the performers take off their masks, the spirits are returned to their bodies, and they have no memory of the ritual.

Jo Riley explains that the physical training for Beijing opera begins with a process of emptying. She posits that the actors have a dual role as exorcists and as performers. In order to fully embody the theatrical and religious rolls they are playing, they must be empty. My experience studying Noh dance-theater in Japan is a direct parallel. I learned two *shimai*, which are slow solo dance songs. When we were performing, we were instructed to be as empty as possible. It was explained that a seasoned performer is sometimes empty enough that the actual spirit of that particular dance will descend the tree painted at the back of the stage and enter the performer. The movements of Northern Shaolin, which I began learning at the age of ten, also share the same basic training with Beijing opera.

Calligraphy can be understood in the same way; it developed in a world where mediumship was common. To learn calligraphy is to copy the exact calligraphic movements of a righteous, accomplished ancestor. Orthodox calligraphy is actually based on one specific government official's style from the sixth century. When beginning to write, the first step is to become empty. From emptiness, one meditates on the ink, the blank piece of paper, and then on the piece of writing to be copied. The brush is held by a body empty of tension; the brushstrokes express the heart/mind *(xin)* while simultaneously transforming it. Whether the calligraphy has an artistic purpose or is used to write talismans, its potency is the direct result of the artist's or priest's ability to empty. From emptiness the characters are manifested internally before being committed to paper. The embodied potency of emptiness is thus transmitted through the image to those who see the writing—informing, inspiring, protecting, purifying, transforming, or healing them, depending on whether the work is talismanic or expressive.

In a similar vein, marionette puppetry performances are considered the most potent of all forms of ritual exorcism, because carved wooden puppets are truly empty. Recounting his research in Taiwan, Kristopher Schipper described Daoist puppet exorcisms which were thought to be so potent, and frighteningly real, that when the beginning of the performance was announced, the entire village would go home and lock their doors and windows.[33] The puppet masters and musicians were the only witnesses. These performers—including Schipper, who learned to

---

33 Kristofer Schipper,. *The Taoist Body*. Univ of California Press, 1993.

play the flute for these shows—all practiced cultivating emptiness so that they would not become possessed. Exorcisms are done to rectify the cosmic order on behalf of a living constituency or the recently dead. The main distinction between an orthodox Daoist exorcism and a lesser exorcism is the ability of the priests to remain empty while invoking and enlisting various potent unseen forces, gods, demons, and spirits.

Earlier we discussed the distinction between internal and external martial arts. There is another way to think about that distinction. With external martial arts, the body is trained to be tough enough to survive the spontaneous and dangerous experience of being possessed. With internal martial arts, emptiness is preserved as a defense against becoming possessed, and as a type of potency for managing chaotic forces. The internal martial artist's spirit *(shen)* becomes the puppet master; his physical body, and the bodies of his adversaries, become like empty puppets on a stage. The spirit (the spatial imagination) controls the strings.

Zhenwu or Xuanwu

The god Zhenwu (the Perfected Warrior) is a central figure in Daoist cosmology; there were countless temples dedicated to him all over China. Before being canonized, Zhenwu was called Xuanwu (Mysterious Warrior). They are sometimes considered different gods, though their iconography is similar. In Taiwan I visited a two story Zhenwu temple, Xuanwu was on the ground floor and Zhenwu was on the top floor. On the walls were murals depicting his many battles. In his theatrical canonization ritual *Journey to the North (Beiyouji)*, it is recounted that after many years of practicing meditation on Mount Wudang, he finally became an immortal when he cut out his internal organs, thereby becoming literally and symbolically empty. The story doesn't end there: after cutting out his internal organs, Xuanwu buried them and forgot about them. But after a few years, they came back to life and grew powerful; his stomach turned into a turtle demon and his intestines turned into a snake demon. These demons became so sexually excited that they decided to go to a nearby village and kidnap a couple of young women, whom they brought back to their cave for sex. When Xuanwu was informed of this, he returned to fight and subdue them. He is thus depicted with one foot on a turtle and one foot on a snake, which entwined together are the ancient symbols of the north.

Emptiness is a key metaphor which operates in a wide variety of contexts. It is found in the foundation texts of many aspects of Chinese culture: Daoist, Buddhist, Confucian, literary, military, musical, and medical. The meaning of emptiness can change as it traverses the strata of society, times, and places. In martial arts, emptiness is the basis, the ground, and the root of action. We should expect the forms to be empty.

We should expect to feel nothing, to taste blandness, see darkness, and hear silence. Emptiness is the most important concept in martial arts, full stop. One's ability to be empty is directly applicable to one's martial skill.

Conclusion

This chapter has covered the ways in which religion is intertwined with martial arts, including conduct, talismans, brotherhoods, the power of *yin*, exorcism, and emptiness. Now we will look at some specific examples.

Figure 20. Zhenwu from *Precious Scripture of the Jade Pivot (Yushu jing)*. Yuan period, dated 1333. Accordion-folded, woodblock-printed book. Courtesy of the British Library.

The Martial Path to Enlightenment

Daoyin

Human life flows within bounds, knowledge has no limits. Using what has limits to pursue what has no limits is exhausting. Knowing this and continuing to pursue knowledge will surely shorten your life. So, regardless of what kind of name you make for yourself, dodge the punishments, stay close to your own center, nourish your body, care for the people around you, and be alive!

—*Zhuangzi*

Daoyin is an ancient physical practice that refines the body toward becoming an immortal *(xian)*. It offers a novel perspective on the purpose of martial arts because it predates martial arts. Fifteen hundred years ago, it included all the elements of martial arts— *except* for martial and theatrical skills. So martial arts can be understood as a style of *daoyin* that has been mixed with theatrical and martial skills. *Daoyin* is the religious core of martial-arts movement training, the root. In its most basic form, it is the physical manifestation of Daoist precepts, refined appetites and an expression of *jindan* (the golden elixir) practice. *Daoyin* incorporated theater and fighting skills because they were such great ways of expressing the fruition of *daoyin* practice—they demonstrate success on the immortal path.[34] *(Watch videos of three different styles of Daoyin.)*[35]

Before giving some historical and contextual background, allow me to describe my own experience. I learned an old seated form of Zhengyidao (orthodox Daoist) *daoyin* from my Daoist teacher Liu Ming.[36] It is done on the ground, and involves pounding, bouncing, rolling, slapping, rubbing, and scraping. It is rough. It is also taught as an interlude between long periods of sitting still, or more accurately sitting and forgetting *(zuowang)*.

Sitting and forgetting is the core practice of religious Daoism; it underlies everything because it is how emptiness is established. But some of us are more restless than others, so Daoists created another way to attain a parallel experience through movement. The assumption is that being human falls somewhere in between stillness and wildness, and that by playing around at these two extremes we might discover something intrinsic about what we are.

It turns out that a stable experience of emptiness *(xu)* is accessible at both extremes—stillness and wildness. Once it is established or made permanent, some people call this experience enlightenment, and perhaps it is, but it is also just a normal part of Daoist training. Still, I think it is at the core of martial arts and theater and creates a kind of background or stage for creative engagement.

Years after studying with Liu Ming, I learned a style of *daoyin* from Monkey Kung Fu master Paulie Zink that was much more complex and theatrical. It is a martial art, and also functions as training for animal roles in Chinese opera. This style of *daoyin* embodies twenty animals and is much more difficult to learn than the orthodox style. However, all the same elements are there: long periods of stillness alternating with dynamic jumping, pounding, scraping, rolling—in a word, *wildness*. The framework of training is built around five distinct qualities of movement: wood, fire, earth, metal, water. They transform the body from the insideout using visualization and playfulness.[37]

---

34   Also see Scott P. Phillips and Daniel Mroz, "Daoyin Reimagined: A Comparison of Three Embodied Traditions," Published in *Journal of Daoist Studies 9* (2016).

35   Daoyin videos: https://goo.gl/x5z1av

36   This practice is quite different from the various types of *qigong* that are also called *daoyin*. Most of those developed out of a social religious movement called "Qigong Fever" in China during the late 1980s and early 1990s. See David A. Palmer, *Qigong Fever: Body, Science, and Utopia in China*. Columbia University Press, 2013.

37   Scott P. Phillips and Daniel Mroz, "Daoyin Reimagined: A Comparison of Three Embodied Traditions," Published in *Journal of Daoist Studies 9* (2016).

The reason this kind of training ended up in the theater is that the end result of all *daoyin* is spontaneity and the complete animation of the body. Those are handy things for a performer to have. *Daoyin* is asocial; it brings out our most wildly inappropriate movement, it opens up cavities in our bodies, loosens our sense of self, and disorients the body we feel. It replaces the hard reality of what we think our body is with an active imagination.

Figure 21. Daoyin: Fire-Frog. 2014. Photo: Daniel Mroz.

For instance, learning the "cat" involves moving and breathing like a frightened cat, taking on the focused mind and body of a hunting cat, and languidly easing into the sexiness of a purring feline licking the underside of her thigh. The "pig" mimes rolling in mud and tromps around snorting. All the animals are playful demonstrations of the outer edges of *wildness* we humans can manifest.

It is that access to freedom from social constraint that must have appealed to Shaolin monks seeking enlightenment when they incorporated *daoyin* into their discipline. Dominance-oriented social violence is dependent on a kind of loss of self-possession, which is the opposite of enlightenment. The physicality of social violence requires communicative tension that says, "I am stronger and more powerful than you are!" and actually causes people to "fight" rather than simply dispatching an aggressor. A person sucked into a fight for social dominance sometimes has trouble taking responsibility. The day after a particularly stupid and avoidable drunken brawl, the participants might say, "The devil made me do it!" (The equivalent in Chinese is "Caocao made me do it!" Caocao was the cruel general who imprisoned the hero Guan Gong in the epic story *The Three Kingdoms*.) The fruition of *daoyin* practice is that it disengages the body from the story of who we (mistakenly) think we are, freeing our physicality. In that sense, the purpose of *daoyin* is to reveal how the limitations of who we think we are (tough, wimpy, righteous, honorable, failure, smart, decent, moral) limit our freedom to act—or not act. Another way to think about this is that the identity we walk around with—the one that likes puppies and tries not to roll our eyes in office meetings—is not the identity one needs access to in a crisis of self-defense. That identity will likely inhibit us from popping an assailant's eardrum with a cupped hand.

Likewise, the expressiveness of a fully animated body is the most important tool of the physically trained performer. Performers need access to fully embodied spontaneity; the capacity to drop *who they are* and become someone else is their stock in trade. Actors must be able to separate their body from their identity. Furthermore, in traditional China, professional performers were in a moral category, a caste, that made them available for sex. They were a type of person considered sexually degraded regardless of whether they actually made a living through prostitution. But to the extent that they did sell sex, the lack of inhibition that *daoyin* instills would have been an asset.

The *daoyin* method achieves these dramatic results by both altering our perception of the body and altering the feeling of the body in space. In both the orthodox and the Paulie Zink styles of *daoyin*, the body is pulled apart and put back together. The felt body is pounded and slapped, altering the sense of where body parts are and how big they are; it is numbed and caressed, flopped and stretched. This creates the sensation of heat radiating out into space. These practices create the feeling that cavities, or empty spaces, are opening up in the torso, and that these spaces connect to the outside world. The limbs become alternately dead weight, flowing water, growing tree limbs, or as hard as stone. The practice is done with visualizations that, over time, come to drive the movement. That is, the feeling of space around the body, which is how we normally orient our bodies in action, is replaced by a wildly active imaginary space. For example, imagine right now that you are in a tub of freezing cold water, and notice how it affects the feeling of your body in space. Now imagine floating on your back in warm mud. This sort of somatic visualization is what drives the movement of *daoyin*. With disciplined, playful practice, *daoyin* effectively replaces both our normatively conditioned habits of movement and our mundane experience of the space we inhabit. The variety of possible visualizations is limitless.

Daoist ritual is one of the important roots of these *daoyin* systems. In rituals, the Daoist priest creates crystal-clear visualizations of deities carrying out actions on behalf of both real and imagined constituencies. These ritual visualizations both drive and enhance the symbolic significance of the priest's ritual movements, dissolving the effort required to make distinctions between real and fake. Likewise, in the theater, visualizations enhance the actors ability to manifest the unseen through skillful movement. Martial artists might be hesitant to accept the idea that visualization is important; after all, to be an effective martial artist, one has to see and feel exactly what is happening. But the confidence with which we hold on to our identities is the first casualty of intimacy with violence. Any profound physical change is accompanied by changes in the way we feel our bodies; the way we feel about ourselves, and the way we feel in space and in the world. The universality of that experience is why *daoyin* has spread and integrated itself into the arts in such a diversity of ways.

Some time before 1500 CE, *daoyin* was used to create the empty-hand martial arts first documented at the Shaolin Temple. During the same period there was an explosion of interest in theater and playwriting. While theater technique was completely undocumented until the twentieth century, *daoyin* was likely incorporated into theater training at about the same time, or perhaps even earlier. It is certainly there now.

It is not known why *daoyin* mixed with fighting and theater at this time. The ethnic diversity that characterized the Yuan dynasty (1279–1368 CE) may have inspired new forms of entertainment; generally dance and music are the first arts to cross a border because they can be understood without a shared language. In addition, countless performing troupes

Figure 22. Vajrapani Painting at Mogao Caves's Hidden Library, Dunhuang, China. Late 9th Century. Courtesy of Wikimedia.

were sent from faraway foreign empires as tribute gifts to China's rulers, likely creating a vibrant milieu for the invention of new and inspiring material. Another factor to consider is that scholars believe the ministers and officials who were loyal to the Mongol dynasty when the Ming dynasty came to power in 1368 were forced to become performers, along with their entire families, in perpetuity, as a punishment in lieu of death that lasted until the twentieth century.[38] These would have been the most educated people in the country, and many were likely familiar with *daoyin*; perhaps some of them even ended up hiding at Shaolin Temple.

Golden Bell and Iron Shirt

The patron deity of Shaolin Temple was Vajrapani, whose name in Sanskrit means "Thunder Hands." His Chinese name is Jingang, which also means diamond: this muscle-bound god perfected his body to the point that it was as hard as diamond, luminous and impenetrable to bladed weapons. As a realized Buddha, Vajrapani's body was a demonstration of his enlightenment. Thus he was a model not only for Shaolin monks practicing meditation, but for numerous character types in the theater and for martial artists everywhere. Because *jingang* means "hard as diamond," it is plausible that it became a general term for describing icons with muscular martial prowess, like the door guardians.[39]

Another image of extraordinary martial prowess sometimes juxtaposed with the impenetrable body is the insubstantial body. The insubstantial body is so fluid and lively that it cannot be touched; it is ghost-like, and bladed weapons appear to pass right through it. This style of prowess is emblematic of the Daoist immortal, or *xian*, of which there are innumerable variations. *Xian* were in some ways similar to gods in that they often had temples dedicated to them, but for Daoist priests and monks, *xian* are models of the unique possibilities each practitioner of self-cultivation can achieve. The insubstantial body was just one possibility.

---

38   Johnson, David George. *Spectacle and Sacrifice: The Ritual Foundations of Village Life in North China*, (2009).p. 227-228. *Also see*, Ye Xiaoqing. "The Legal and social status of theatrical performers in Beijing during the Qing." (2003).
39   Meir Shahar. *The Shaolin Monastery: History, Religion, and the Chinese Martial Arts*. University of Hawaii Press, (2008).

Figure 23. Miming the Door Gods, each holding a hemp rope for tying up demons. (Golden Rooster Stands on One Leg, Posture from Chen style Taijiquan). Photo: Sarah Halverstadt.

The body conditioning practices of Iron Shirt and Golden Bell have a long history in China. For clarity it could be said that Iron Shirt practices strive to achieve the impenetrable diamond body, and Golden Bell practices strive to achieve the insubstantial body. The terms for these two practices were often interchangeable because these two distinct types of fruition are closely related, and both were used in warfare and on the stage.

These practices are also highly developed in *daoyin*, which is possibly the source of their integration and dissemination. However, Meir

Shahar[40] has shown that Iron Shirt and Golden Bell practices existed as far away as India more than a thousand years ago. The notion of the impenetrable body and the insubstantial body were alive in the popular imagination over a long period of time and a huge swath of geography. Both methods draw on notions of emptiness to facilitate body conditioning.

In the case of Iron Shirt, the body is struck while the mind simultaneously compresses *qi*, as imagined breath, at the site of impact, which over time creates a conditioned response to external shock. This feeling of hardening the body is simultaneously imagined (and eventually perceived) as a kind of emptiness *(xu)*. This type of emptiness feels numb and dead, like being a wooden puppet, as if one's body is not one's own. Although the body is desensitized, the stimulation is pleasurable. The body feels larger and is filled with an otherworldly vigor and aliveness. This fairly common effect is part of what makes fighting and training so much fun and such a great bonding experience.

In the case of Golden Bell, the training establishes the feeling of the body as a hollow container that rings out in all directions when it is struck, like a bell. The imagined *qi* in this case is felt as radiating sound or light, so that the sensation of external shock is replaced with a feeling of expansiveness or luminosity. In this case, the experience of emptiness is felt in two ways simultaneously; first, the body becomes a container *(kong)* which does not tense or contract when struck, thus remaining hollow; and second, imagined sound or light radiates out into infinite emptiness *(xu)*.

This experience in popular theatrical religious contexts was called *shenming* (luminosity). The "golden" *(jin)* in Golden Bell and the *"jin"* in Jingang (the Chinese name for Vajrapani) are the same character in Chinese. (The same character is also used in the word *jindan*, the Daoist practice of the golden elixir of immortality) The basic cosmological premise behind the practices of *jindan* and *daoyin* are the same: there is an order of action between *jing, qi,* and *shen*. In stillness *jing* and *qi* distill; that is, they come apart while remaining in contact right next to each other. *Jing*, in its most direct meaning, is the physical mass of the body itself. *Qi*, in its most direct meaning, is the totality of the felt body. So the felt body floats off from the actual substantive body, and they become distinct. The practice of *daoyin*, fully realized, is in fact *jindan* in motion.

---

40   Meir Shahar. "Indian Mythology and the Chinese Imagination: Nezha, Nalakubara, and Krisna." *India in the Chinese Imagination: Myth, Religion, and Thought* (2013)

Both practices reveal an ordered procession of layers, like an egg. *Jing* is the yolk, *qi* is the egg white and *shen* (felt space) is the shell radiating out into emptiness *(xu)*. Or, to use the bell metaphor, *jing* is the metal surrounded by emptiness, *qi* is the vibration, and *shen* is the sound.

A core experience of most martial artists is the delight we take in playing between the polarities of discipline and freedom. Long hours of disciplined practice bear the fruit of increased range of motion, power, and freedom. The difference between the impenetrable body and the insubstantial body parallels the differences between external (hard) and internal (soft) styles of martial arts. Both approaches are just different ways of practicing *daoyin*. Framing martial arts as a form of *daoyin* connects it with deep roots in the Daoist religious experience, and opens doors to new sources of inspiration.

Example of Taijiquan

When I first started learning Chen-style *taijiquan* with George Xu, everything was about martial skills. Every inch of the form had at least three techniques, including striking, throwing, and breaking. Chen style *taijiquan* gets its name from a Chen family village called Chenjiagou. Chen style is probably the oldest style of *taijiquan*, from which other styles most likely originated.

At the same time I was studying *kathak*, north Indian dance. In *kathak*, there is a move in which the god Krishna puts away his flute and ties his belt. The mime for tying the belt is almost the same as the end of the *taijiquan* movement called "lazy about tying one's coat." In *taijiquan* it was done on the right side instead of the left, but it was the same right-hand-dominant movement. Of course, the technique had a martial application too—but why was it there at all?

The very name *kathak* means storytelling, and it uses a lot of mime. However, an outsider would not likely know that the three-fingered *mudra* is the god Shiva's trident, or that a narrower variation of the same *mudra* is the god Krishna's peacock feather. I also found the *kathak* hand gesture for "opening the heart in all directions like a lotus flower" (figure 24) in the *taijiquan* movement sequence, although it was done just below the bellybutton instead of at the chest.

For a long time I had no explanation why there was mime in the *taijiquan* form. Yet, because I was working as a dancer and learning choreography skills, I was acutely aware of many performance elements in *taijiquan*.

Figure 24. Opening the Heart in all Directions, Kathak Dance. Photo: Sarah Halverstadt.

There were three major breakthroughs in coming to understand what *taijiquan* is, and many smaller ones along the way. The first lay in understanding that the form told a story. To see that, I first had to understand a great deal about how Daoist ritual is structured, and how Chinese narratives are structured. Finally, I had to figure out the meanings of specific gestures.

The second was recognizing that *taijiquan* is a type of *jindan* (the golden elixir). Once I saw that the narrative was structured like a Daoist ritual, it was easy to conclude that the practice could be done as *jindan*, since Daoist ritual is an elaborate form of it. But it wasn't until George Xu showed me that the martial skills aspect of *taijiquan* was entirely based on *jindan* that I actually saw it. And I didn't actually believe it myself until I could do it, at which point I realized that one purpose of the narrative is to explain how *taijiquan* works.

The third breakthrough came from talking about enlightenment with Rory Miller.[41] I came to see *taijiquan* as a transgressive path to becoming an immortal *(xian)*. These insights developed from thinking about the effects violence has on identity, and how those changes might have shaped the way the movement art developed. The Daoist relationship to violence is counterintuitive and controversial, but taken as a whole, the practice of *taijiquan* can be understood as an expression of Daoist precepts.

---

41   Author of *Meditations on Violence* (Wolfeboro, NH: YMAA Publications, 2008).

Taijiquan **uses theatrical elements and training**

Taijiquan, like all martial arts, was developed to be effectively used for breaking bones and many other violent techniques—and it works! But violent technique is not its primary purpose.

Performance skills are part of *taijiquan* training. Its stances establish body shape and orientation, which allow one to sustain character roles, and develop exaggerated movement for the stage. One of the most important components of physical theater training and dance is the way the body is used in space to effectively control not just where the audience looks but how the audience perceives space on the stage. Movement of the body in *taijiquan* can be used to give an audience the sense that the performer is on a narrow trail in the fog, in a beautiful garden, or perhaps in a large cavernous room. It turns out this has a name in Chinese opera; it is called "wearing the scene on the body," *(jing jiuzai yanyuan shenshang)*.[42]

From a theatrical point of view, the precision with which *taijiquan* is taught is highly functional. It gives the performer a movement position to return to and relax in, a physical exactness from which to improvise.

Traditional Chinese theater uses mime and other spatial movement conventions to communicate time, places, people, and objects—very few props or scenery other than a chair or a table are used. Like Indian dance, Chinese theater uses mime to create illusions, but the main function of mime is its use as a symbolic language. For example, crossed open hands on the left side of the body can symbolize a butterfly, which means "waking from a dream" because—as everyone initiated into this culture of mime would know—the ancient Daoist author Zhuangzi had a dream in which he was a butterfly, and the butterfly had a dream in which he was Zhuangzi, and afterwards Zhuangzi was never quite sure whether he was himself or a butterfly. "Suddenly, waking from a dream" is a Chinese theatrical convention used extensively to navigate plotlines between other worlds, ghost realms, alternate futures, enlightenment, disillusionment, or simply waking up in hell. Realizing that the butterfly mime was in the *taijiquan* form, and had been a widely recognized convention, was a watershed moment for me. I have come to see Chen-style *taijiquan*, particularly its silk-reeling power *(chansijin)*, as advanced training for mime. It creates the ability to spiral and rotate not just the wrists and fingers, but any part of the body; the training generates a

---

42   Yung Sai-shing, "Moving Body: The Interactions Between Chinese Opera and Action Cinema," in *Hong Kong Connections: Transnational Imagination in Action Cinema*, 2005.

lively quality of movement with which to improvise, allowing all the articulation points in the body to float.

Most of the movement names in the Chen-style form (and hundreds of other martial-arts forms) are images from religious theater. The postures themselves also inhabit a character type, used most often to play martial gods, generals, and judges, known as the "painted face," or sometimes the "beard" because these characters often have a long flowing beard. Beard-manipulation mime is prominent in the *taijiquan* form.[43]

There is a lot of theatrical training in Chen-style *taijiquan*, mostly it needs to be seen and felt, and what can be easily written about is covered elsewhere in this book in the section on theatricality in the martial arts, so I won't repeat myself here.

Taijiquan tells a story, the story of its own creation

Around the thirteenth century there was an internal alchemist, a master of *jindan* named Zhang Sanfeng, living on Wudang Mountain. We don't know much about the actual man, but stories and theatrical material created about his magical powers were ubiquitous. He was also channeled extensively by spirit-writing cults over several hundred years, and is credited with transmitting many Daoist practices. The oldest written account that associates Zhang Sanfeng with an internal school of martial arts was on an epitaph honoring a member of the gentry who passively resisted the new Qing dynasty sometime after its establishment in 1644. The epitaph explains that there are external martial arts transmitted through Shaolin Temple and there are internal martial arts transmitted through Zhang Sanfeng.

The epitaph is the earliest known version of the following story, which is familiar to many in *taijiquan* circles:

In a dream, Zhang Sanfeng met with the martial god Xuanwu, who revealed the art of taijiquan to him. (Xuanwu's name means "mysterious-dark warrior.") Zhang Sanfeng then woke up, went outside, and saw a crane and a snake fighting. As he watched these lively animals, he saw that no matter how hard each tried, neither the crane nor the snake could catch the other one. This reminded him of the art he had learned in the dream, and he began to practice it. Shortly after that he

---

43   This is distinct from Northern Shaolin forms, which usually inhabit the youthful warrior or the comic character roles.

was called to the capital by the emperor. As Zhang Sanfeng was making his way to the capital, he was attacked by a hundred bandits. Using the art he had learned from Xuanwu, he singlehandedly defeated all the bandits. Zhang Sanfeng later passed this art on to worthy disciples, and became a Daoist immortal (xian).[44][45]

A temple dedicated to Zhang Sanfeng was located near Wudang Mountain, not far Chen Village.[46] People went there to make offerings of incense to Zhang Sanfeng and probably to ask for blessings from the immortal. Immortals are treated by popular temple culture in much the same way gods are treated; in practice they often serve the same functions. Immortals are the embodiment of everything being okay the way it is; whereas Chinese gods are more likely to have an agenda. Both can be variously righteous, benevolent, compassionate, tricky, or just having a good time. The idea that gods or immortals have a sense of humor was a common element of Chinese temple religion. At that temple, there was a statue of the immortal Zhang Sanfeng with a large metal gong on his head, which he wore instead of a straw hat. People who visited the temple would go up and bang the gong, hitting the statue on the head. Naturally, it would ring loudly, allowing "Zhang Sanfeng" to demonstrate his good nature and equanimity—by doing nothing at all. This doing nothing, called *wuwei* in Chinese, is the central subject of Daoism's most sacred text, the *Daodejing*.

The idea that *taijiquan* might come from Zhang Sanfeng is angrily disputed by some modern practitioners and historians, and is contrary to the official government line. Historically speaking, however, the art of *taijiquan* comes out of this region where the cult to Zhang Sanfeng was strong and people had a sense of humor. The first style of *taijiquan* to come to public attention was Yang style. It was taught in the capital by a man named Yang Luchan in the late 1800s. In the early twentieth century a short collection of texts about *taijiquan* were published; these were probably written around 1860 by the Wu brothers: Yuxiang, Zhuqing and Chengqing, who were members of the gentry class. Most

44   Translated by Douglas Wile with minor changes. *Lost T'ai-chi Classics from the Late Ch'ing Dynasty*. SUNY Press, 1996, p. 26.

45   Douglas Wile suggests that this epitaph was more of a political allegory about Chinese (i.e., internal and Daoist) ways being better than foreign ones (Shaolin Temple's Buddhism having originated in India and the new rulers of the Qing Dynasty being from north of the Great Wall). Regardless of the meaning of the epitaph, the idea of Zhang Sanfeng as the progenitor of an internal martial art must have existed at the time this was written, ca. 1700.

46   Wile, 1996, p. 110.

accounts agree that Wu Yuxiang studied *taijiquan* under Yang Luchan, who had learned the art while working as a bonded servant in Chen Village.[47] We have no way of knowing how widespread the art was in the region around Chen Village or how many people in the village practiced it. But one man named Chen Fake arrived in Beijing in the 1920s and started teaching Chen-style *taijiquan*. This is where most of the modern versions of Chen style come from, including the one I practice.

The Chen-Style *Taijiquan* Form as Dramatic Storytelling

What follows is a step-by-step analysis of the beginning of the Chen-style *taijiquan* form as storytelling. (Watch the video.)[48]

The opening movement in the Chen style *taijiquan* form, raising and lowering the arms, is a standardized movement in theatrical contexts meaning, "start the music," much as a conductor in Western classical music would hold up a baton. This musical beginning parallels the way in which music is used at the beginning of Daoist rituals to invoke the world coming into existence from *hundun* (undifferentiated chaos) in which land rises out of the oceans (figures 25 & 26). *Hundun* is represented by water moving in ten directions simultaneously, and is often depicted on the bottom fringe of Daoist vestments.

The second movement is called "play the *pipa*." The meaning of *pipa* here is multilayered, creating a picture that comes in and out of focus. First it is a four-stringed musical instrument, the plucking of which makes the sounds "pi" and "pa." It is also the sound of breaking bones— the direct equivalent of the word "crack" in English. Furthermore, the scapula bone is also called the *pipa*. The earliest writing in China, called "oracle bones," were sheep's scapulas which were "cracked" with a hot poker and then read as divinations from the gods, which were then carved into the bones. This is why, during the Tang Dynasty (618–907), female fortunetellers were called "*pipa* diviners." In the Chen-style form, the "playing the *pipa*" movement is the invocation of the iconic female shaman (figure 27). In Daoist cosmology, ancient shamans are the access point, if not the source, of the gods who come later in history.

---

47   Douglas Wile, *Lost T'ai-chi Classics from the Late Ch'ing Dynasty* (Syracuse, NY: SUNY Press), 17–19.
48   Watch "The Cultural History of Tai Chi" the video at Youtube.com/c/NorthStarMartialArtsUSA

Figure 25. Huntun (totally undifferentiated chaos) shown on Imperial clothing, mid-1700s. From, Field Museum of Natural History, Annual Report 1921. Courtesy of Wikimedia.

Figure 26. Start the Music

Figure 27. Water emerges from hundun, and Play the Pipa. Photos: Sarah Halverstadt.

The movement may also be a comic reference to a folk punishment for public fighting, which was to break the combatants' scapula bones.

Daoist ritual masters transform from one icon or deity to another, and then to another, in succession as intermediaries used to approach *the Dao*.

The next movement, which is usually not named, relates to the ancestor of all male shamans, Da Yu,[49] who is half-man and half-bear (because he married a bear) (figure 29). He is invoked because he unifies the nine kingdoms and tames the waters so that civilization—and thus the gods—can come into existence. He slumps to one side, drags his foot, and stamps the ground to disperse *yin* spirits.

Figure 28. Land emerging from water.

Figure 29. Da Yu half-man half-bear.

Figure 30. Jingang Pounds the Mortar.

The third movement is called "Jingang pounds the mortar," (*Jingang dadui* in Chinese). Jingang is the formal name for the *vajra* or diamond guardians of the Buddha, but in popular culture probably referred to any martial deity or immortal with superhuman strength (figure 30). The movement itself embodies the character role known as "painted-face" used for generals and judges. Directly after the pounding action, this character grinds the ingredients and then drinks them. In the logic of the narrative, this is none other than Xuanwu (the Mysterious Warrior); he is making and drinking the elixir of immortality (figures 31 & 32) (for an image of Xuanwu *see figure 20)*.

---

49   Some Daoist rituals use Pangu instead of Da Yu in this role. Pangu, who wears a bearskin, created the lands and forests from his body.

Figure 31. Xuanwu mixing the elixir of Immortality.

The next movement, "lazy about tying the coat" is immediately preceded by a flipping of the open palms into the shape of a butterfly (figure 33). This gesture means "waking from a dream" in Chinese vernacular storytelling, a reference to Zhuangzi, as mentioned above. Next, a figure in horse stance draws his fingers down the front of his body and makes a circling motion at the belly, opening the fingers one by one (figure 34). This circling movement is nearly identical to the mime used in north Indian dance in front of the chest to mean "opening the heart in all directions" (figure 24). As simple mime, this part of the form communicates the concept of "sinking the *qi* to the *dantian* and releasing

Wen and Wu

Chinese culture uses the terms *wen* (civil) and *wu* (martial) to differentiate innumerable things; the term is perhaps even more commonly used than *yin* and *yang*. For instance, all officers of the court were divided into *wen* and *wu*, as were all male gods in the vast cosmology and all theatrical plays, and all character roles in those plays. The gongs, especially the dissonant gongs, were considered *wu*; the drum was considered *wen*. *Wu* is the forces of chaos in the cosmos; *wen* is the forces of order in the cosmos. In martial-arts classes we begin and end by covering the fist *(wu)* with the open palm *(wen)*, symbolically stating our commitment to develop maximum explosive power *(wu)* and the ability to control it *(wen)*.

Without *wu*, everything would die. It is vigor, it is spontaneity, it is passion. Without *wu*, nothing could ever experience renewal. But without *wen*, there would be no sense of home, safety, or ease.

Hundun and Taiji

The term *hundun*, which roughly translates to "totally undifferentiated chaos," includes everything. There is just as much order in *hundun* as there is chaos, just as much *wen* as there is *wu*. It contains all things, but they are undifferentiated so it is impossible to distinguish between them. Up and down are there, but one doesn't experience them as distinct.

Taijiquan gets its name from *taiji* as a cosmological concept. *Taiji* is that moment, place, existence of infinite potential—the gateway to manifestation. But it is equally that emptiness and non-being of infinite destruction—the gateway where all things dissolve and die. Together, these flow between meaning and meaninglessness, between beginnings and endings, between knowing and not knowing.

In Daoist ritual, *Dao* is zero, *hundun* is one, *taiji* is two, and three is *wanwu*, the infinite possibilities manifest (literally, "ten thousand things"). *Hundun* is the closest a human can come to experiencing *Dao; taiji* is two steps out of the abyss.

Figure 32. Drinking the Elixir.

Figure 33. Butterfly, "Waking from a dream."

its power in all directions." But a humorous interpretation might also be miming the ribbons of office hanging down the front of the torso, and then tying up the pants. This is none other than Zhang Sanfeng, having waken from a dream of Xuanwu cultivating the golden elixir and then getting dressed.

The next movement mimes putting on a large hat (figure 35) and then stroking a beard. The hat is Zhang Sanfeng's signature straw hat, and his beard is said to be the shape of a halberd blade with gleaming silver whiskers. Zhang then ties his belt (figure 36). Again, the mime here is very similar to that used in north Indian dance, where tying a belt is commonly used to convey the god Krishna tying his flute to his waist.[50]

---

50   Zhang Sanfeng is often described as carrying a cylindrical "ruler" which is basically a magic wand used for exorcism. Perhaps he is tying *this* up in his belt.

Figure 34. Zhang Sanfeng ties up his pants, and expands his *dantian* in all directions.

Figure 35. Zhang Sanfeng puts on his hat and strokes his halberd shaped beard

Next is "single whip" which begins with a stroking of the beard and the lifting of the leg into the air. In Beijing Opera *(jingju)*, this movement (figure 36) is used to present a new character entering the stage. The term "single-whip" *(danbian)* refers to a pole with a rope tied to one

Figure 36. Zhang Sanfeng ties his belt and steps outside.

Figure 37. Where he sees...a snake...and a crane fighting.

end—called a whipping in nautical parlance—used for loading and unloading baskets from a boat. One of the most distinctive principles of *taijiquan* is the use of the body as a counterbalance to external forces, rather than using force directly against force. "Single-whip" is a symbolic representation of a counterbalance as a movement principle. Simultaneously, the hand reaching out in the direction of the gaze mimes looking out into the distance and seeing something (figure 37).

And what is it that Zhang Sanfeng would be seeing? The next move, called "white crane spreads its wings," shows a snake and then a crane. This is followed by a movement called "brush knee," in which one hand chases the other, repeated three times. This mimes a crane and a snake taking turns chasing each other (figure 38).

What is the *dantian*, and where is it located?

The term *dantian*, which means "elixir field," suggests the place where the golden elixir is cultivated. However, that "place" is not a place—it is emptiness. It has a parallel in the consecrated stage or temple, which has been ritually emptied. In meditation it is both the beginning and the end; meditation practice is the designation of time and place one returns to over and over. As a teaching convention, the *dantian* has various symbolic locations; in *taijiquan* it is the lower part of the torso, the belly, which functions as a starting place. But in practice, the *dantian* is the field of perceptual imagination, the source of balance and coordination. Thus, in *taijiquan* practice, circling the *dantian* corresponds to creating a new order of action, making the internal larger than the external, by connecting emptiness inside to movement outside the body. *Dan*, which refers to the elixir, literally means "cinnabar-red," the color of blood. Thus, *dantian* also implies the metaphor of turning the body inside out on the altar of emptiness.

Figure 38. One hand represents the crane, the other the snake. As the snake and the crane fought, neither one could catch the other, seeing this, he recalled his dream of Xuanwu, and the *taijiquan* principle of a counter-balance. He then went on to battle 100 bandits using this art.

All variants of the first Chen-style form *(yilu)* that I'm aware of follow this pattern up to here. Some forms then repeat "Jingang pounds the mortar" and execute another "single-whip," and some forms have an additional movement of a butterfly moving in a complete circle.

Following the storyline, Zhang Sanfeng then sets off on a journey through the mountains and goes on to fight a hundred bandits. As all *taijiquan* movements can easily be conceptualized as mimed fighting; the whole rest of the form could simply be Zhang Sanfeng fighting the bandits, thus making a substantive display of his immortal treasures.

Further Analysis of the Story

The rest of the form contains many different *taijiquan* posture names. Some of these are from popular theater, like "needle in the bottom of

Figure 39. A counter-balance. (Single-whip.)

the sea," which is a reference to Sun Wukong taking a pillar from the palace of the Dragon King at the bottom of sea. After using it as a fighting staff, Sun Wukong magically shrinks it and puts it behind his ear and gives it the name "needle." "Fair lady works the shuttles," mimes the expression form the epic *Journey to the North*, "The sun and the moon rose and fell like the shuttles of a loom," which means—a lot of time passing. "Golden cock stands on one leg" mimes the two Door Gods greeting the morning sun. (See figure 23.) They protect the sacred peach tree on which the Golden Cock roosts. And "seven-star punch" mimes the Big Dipper, which points to the North Star, around which all the other stars rotate. Each star in the sky represents a possible fate, thus the North Star is the "pivot point" of all fates. For this reason the seven stars of the dipper are routinely invoked as a powerful weapon used in exorcisms.

We don't know yet what the exact significance and meaning of each of these movement phrases is, but the overall story is about ritual transformation. Zhang Sanfeng travels amongst the stars, which are gods and immortals in various stages of returning to the *Dao*. The ritual ends with Zhang Sanfeng's canonization as an immortal. Zhang, comically, has to fight all these celestials in order to attain his canonization. That is, the hundred bandits are immortals, gods, and demons, who are accumulating merit through righteous combat. This formal structure of fiction-as-exorcism is characteristic of the Chinese literary tradition.[51][52]

Taijiquan as embodied *jindan* and cosmology

In addition to the external theatrical elements, the *taijiquan* form embodies Daoist internal alchemy, jindan. In its simplest form, *jindan* is tracking the intrinsic flow of *qi* up the back and down the front while connecting that flow to the movements of the cosmos. In its most complex ritual form, it is connecting the totality of the felt body to processions of time, changes in the environment, and to the entirety of the unseen realms of immortals, gods, and ghosts.

Jindan uses iconic visualizations to relate our immediate experience to *ziran*—the spontaneous and continuous self-reproducing nature of things. *Jindan* is the practice of living in a spontaneously animated world, unconstrained by anything other than the way things are, unfixed and ambiguous. It is potency unattached to a fixed identity.

Taijiquan postures are typically held for long periods of time. *Jindan* practices begin in stillness. Beginning *taijiquan* in stillness effortlessly invokes the experience of *zuowang*, "sitting and forgetting." As a non-conceptual practice, this type of stillness has no up or down, no set size

---

51   See, for instance, Mark R. E. Meulenbeld, *Demonic Warfare: Daoism, Territorial Networks, and the History of a Ming Novel,* University of Hawaii Press, 2015.

52   Another possibility is that he tricks all these adversaries into fighting each other. That idea comes from a play in which Zhang Sanfeng is featured—Chapter 57 of *Zheng He's Journey to the West by Boat (Sanbao taijian xia xiyangji)*(1597). (Thanks to Marnix Wells for help with the translation.)

or position, it is by definition undefined. However, relative to movement, the experience can take shape as a feeling of space. Relative to upright movement, it can feel like a huge stage, an empty space where actions sensed corporeally and imagined can take place. This spatial experience of emptiness is called the establishment of the *dantian*.[53]

Once this ritual platform of spatial awareness is established, the body is moved indirectly by the visualization of natural forces outside the body. To achieve this effect, the physical body must be completely empty *(xu)*. Any intent *(yi)* which enters the body will cause it to become full. The experience of the body being empty in motion arises gradually as both effort and intent are discarded. One might call this discarding desire, but it is more specific than that; it is the practice of not initiating action from within the body.

This experience of *xu* is a deep form of relaxation commonly experienced by people drifting off to sleep. It can also arise spontaneously after very intense emotional experiences, like fear or cathartic dancing, or it may be induced by drugs; however, in those situations it tends to feel like a loss of body orientation or perception—a kind of numbness. Once emptiness is established in motion, imagination replaces the feeling of the body. In *taijiquan* teaching paradigms, structural integrity and coordination of the body are trained extensively before these practices are attempted.

There are an infinite number of ways of practicing *jindan*. In the one I practice, from "sitting and forgetting," one visualizes the martial deity Zhenwu, and then becomes Zhenwu. As Zhenwu, one visualizes Laojun Daode (the deified Laozi) surrounded by rainbows, and then becomes him. Zhenwu is a militarily disciplined character, whereas Laojun is babylike, waterlike, spontaneous, and has no inhibition. It is important to understand that this practice is part of *taijiquan*, but I'm leaving out most of the details because this cannot be learned from a book; it requires a direct transmission from teacher to student.

Once the action of *jindan* begins, perfect visualization is identical to the practice of emptying, because the substantive body is completely transformed into an imagined one. What one visualizes is less important than that the image is active and spatially alive. For example, Zhenwu's skin is infinitely deep and dark like the night sky. The god Xuanwu also has skin infinitely deep and dark like the night sky, so in *taijiquan* practice

---

53   The term *dantian* is often used in Chinese martial arts contexts to mean 'the center of the body' or 'the center of coordination,' but literally it translates as "cinnabar field," a clear reference to a platform on which rituals of transformation are performed.

the visualizations of these two gods are functionally interchangeable. In fact, Zhenwu is the canonized version of Xuanwu. (See the sidebar note in the Martial Theater as Exorcism subchapter.)

Laojun Daode is similarly interchangeable with Zhang Sanfeng, visualized living on Mount Wudang among subtle mists and rainbows. These visualizations are in effect the enactment of a list of spatially imagined infinite qualities, like armor gleaming out in all directions, or a halberd-shaped beard made of gleaming silver whiskers.

There is symmetry between the *taijiquan* story of Zhang Sanfeng having a dream and the practice of *jindan* as ritual visualization. In the *taijiquan* story we go from pure *qi* emerging from *hundun* as light and music and then taking substantive form as emergent *jing*: first water and then land. This is followed by the appearance of the ancestor of female shamans and then Da Yu, half-man, half-bear, who uses his wild side, his bear side, to stamp the ground—bringing the world into order by sending *yin* spirits downward. Suddenly Da Yu is transformed *(bianhua)* into Xuanwu, and then into Zhang Sanfeng. In the story, Zhang Sanfeng experiences this as a dream, because he is practicing *jindan* as a Daoist dream practice traditionally called "making day and night the same."[54] *Taijiquan* is, of course, well known for its dreamlike movement.

Everything I have written about so far is a single integrated practice. The *fruition* of that practice can be performed theatrically, expressed as martial prowess, or simply lived as spontaneous authenticity.

Violence as a Transgressive Path to Enlightenment

The story of Zhang Sanfeng fighting all these bandits makes a connection between adept execution of violence and becoming an immortal. This notion that experiences with violence can lead to enlightenment or anything personally or socially positive is a profoundly transgressive one in most contemporary societies. There is nonetheless a slowly accumulating body of evidence which supports this view. The problem in trying to understand what role experiences of violence might play in a transgressive path to enlightenment is the simple fact that most of us live in relative safety. A martial artist rarely has substantial experience with violence outside of social challenges and

---

54   Dream practice is a subject for another book; however, Tibetan Dzogchen has the same approach to dream. See *Dream Yoga and the Practice of Natural Light*, by Chogyal Namkhai Norbu, Snow Lion, 2002.

competitive bouts. To gain insights in this realm, I refer readers to the ideas of Rory Miller, author of *Meditations on Violence*. Miller writes about accumulating hundreds of documented uses of force while working in criminal corrections and officer training.

Experience with violence can wound people emotionally, but it can also lead to emotional maturity and it can make people stronger. Violent encounters release a cocktail of hormones into the blood stream via the endocrine system, popularly called an adrenaline rush—because of the rushing sound it can make in the ears. With repeated experiences of violence some people can become accustomed to the "rush" such that they can distinguish it from emotional reactions, freeing them to act rationally.

Violent face to face social challenges—what Miller calls "the Monkey Dance"—are a universal and highly predictable form of emotionally driven violence. Social violence has a fundamentally different "logic of violence" than asocial violence. Most asocial violence is focused on acquiring resources (like muggings) and avoiding witnesses. Social violence typically requires an audience. Extensive experience with asocial violence can lead an individual to lose the psycho-physiological-social triggers which normally drive social violence. This can awaken the ability to clearly distinguish between social and asocial violence, facilitating the freedom to act decisively and rationally in the midst of violent chaos when everyone else is freaking out. This outcome can be understood as the ability to transcend earthly passions and the distractions of social obligations, constraints, and conventions.

Extreme experiences of violence can lead to an "every day above ground is a good day" sort of positive fatalism, or to the feeling that *mundane everyday life offers no real stimulation.* As Rory Miller puts it, the first casualty of a violent encounter is one's identity. The identities we inhabit—being kind, generous and polite, for example—are not capable of violent action, so they must be transcended if such action is to be taken. Even just witnessing extreme horror can destroy the part of one's identity that is tied to an idea about the way the world is, resulting in either a retreat from reality or profound identity readjustment.

Being free of the connection between the adrenaline rush and conflicting emotions can lead a person to the realization that morality is a conscious choice. Not everyone who has extensive experiences with violence becomes enlightened, of course. But experiences of violence can be understood as a transgressive step along a road to immortal transcendence. The idea that violent characters have access to enlightenment is one of the dominant themes of Chinese theater. The immortal Zhang Sanfeng, as a character in the theater, was able to fight multiple opponents in his sleep. Sun Wukong fights his way to enlightenment in *Journey to the West*, so does Xuanwu in *Journey to the North*. Simultaneously, that connection was instilled in the popular imagination through arts like *taijiquan*.

Example of Shaolin

Buddhist monks portrayed on the stage were either enlightened, evil, or somewhere in the process of becoming one or the other. This was an entertaining subject for the theater, and it was through the theater that most people knew about Shaolin Monastery as a place where monks had great martial skills. Everyone saw fighting monks on the stage in their local village. There is an epic collection of these plays called *Crazy Ji the Mad Monk*.[55]

Shaolin kung fu (also called Shaolin Quan) gets its name from Shaolin Temple, a Chan Buddhist monastery where Shaolin has been practiced for at least six hundred years. Shaolin Quan (*quan* means fist or art, *lin* means forest) is another example of how martial arts were fully integrated in theater and religion. Shaolin is a big category that doesn't refer to any single art. It is often used as a synonym for "external" martial arts.[56]

Shaolin Temple was located on a key strategic pass on Mount Song. What that meant in terms of its involvement in the long history of conflict and dynastic changes is beyond the scope of this book, but the monks certainly developed a reputation for martial prowess. Scattered across the ages there are accounts of a hundred or so monks here or there participating in military battles, a small but symbolic presence. However, if we consider that individual monks travelled from Shaolin to the countless other Chan Buddhist temples scattered around China, it is likely that as individuals they often played a role in training locals for village defense or the creation of militias.

---

55   Guo Xiaoting. *Adventures of the Mad Monk Ji Gong*. Trans. John Robert Shaw. Into. Victoria Cass. Tuttle, 2014.

56   Shaolin literally means "small forest" it is related to the term *wulin* (martial forest) used in contemporary film and fiction to describe an imaginary world of exceptional martial prowess. The more traditional term *jianghu* (lakes & rivers) means the same thing but implies more magical forms of kung fu. This contemporary distinction follows the modern discourse in creatively rewriting cultural history to include notions of *pure* martial arts. The *Crazy Ji* epic uses a variation of this term *lulin* (green forest). See *War, Humiliation, and "Pure" Martial Arts*, in the next section.

The first accounts of fighting monks come from literature. They are stories of monks drinking, fornicating, eating meat, and of course, getting in lots of fights. Most likely the written literature came from street performers, who no doubt acted out the fun bits. Over time the idea of the transgressive monk found its way into theater as a stock character. Since Buddhist monks with awesome fighting skills appeared on the stage earlier than the first accounts of monks training for combat at Shaolin Temple, this may have been a case of life imitating art. Regardless of where it showed up first, there has been a continuous mutual influence between the monks of the theater and monks of the temple. Down through the ages, monks were *wuxia* (martial heroes). Nearly all the important *wuxia* recorded by history were popularized through the theater; that is how people knew about them. The monks of Shaolin Temple are perhaps the most famous of all. They have spread their arts all over China—and now the world—with the enlightened goal of spreading harmony.

In practice, the term Shaolin covers a wide range of styles and practices. Bruce Lee taught a form of southern Shaolin. I learned a style of northern Shaolin that other schools sometimes refer to as Islamic Long Fist, probably because the first form taught in my school is a version of tantui (springy legs) that was widely taught among the Hui, a Muslim ethnic group that historically had been enlisted as cavalries for the Chinese military. Yet the *tantui* I learned not only has theatrical elements in it, it is in fact Chinese opera training; albeit with an emphasis on toughness. I didn't realize this when I was learning it, but the basic warmups we did for Northern Shaolin are the character roles used in Chinese opera. These are, in order: *sheng* (scholarly lead character), painted face (generals and judges), *chou* (comics), *wu* (young warrior prince/princess).

The basic stances are platforms for character roles. The final leg stretch is called chin-to-toe. In the opera, before going on the stage a performer would put on costume and makeup and then wait in the chin-to-toe position until they got their cue to go on stage. The kicks we learned were stage-ready, with such rhythmic precision that the tops of our kicks went above our heads on the up-beat, often accompanied by foot-slapping percussion. Although the sequence of movements I learned are not the same as the arts currently coming out of Shaolin Temple, it is clearly the same art; the stances and techniques are the same.

I've been teaching Northern Shaolin as a performing art to children, with gongs, wood blocks, and drums for more than twenty years. I

Figure 40. Basic Shaolin stances and their expressions.

use it as a platform for teaching physical theater, improvisation, and imparting moral virtues like self-direction and personal responsibility. My teacher's teacher, Kuo Lien-ying, practiced Monkey Style, and sang songs from the opera which he had learned in his youth, but he never made any claims about the art having a connection to theater. Nor did he make any claims about its religious content, yet he practiced standing meditation for an hour every day without fail. His rope-dart techniques were renowned, and he never taught them to anyone; he never found a student worthy enough. He said that he used his rope-dart when he was a bodyguard in Shanghai, and many of his students remember being tied up in an instant. The rope-dart is a highly theatrical weapon, and according to his own account, the most practical one.

My own experience of practicing Shaolin has religious meaning. In my school it was always preceded by an hour of standing still meditation, a practice with no instruction other than body structure corrections. That is, in essence, the Chan Buddhist way. This kind of practice changes the way people move, and inspires a kind of morality in motion, a kind of movement efficiency and efficacy; it is self-healing, too. This daily ritual of renewal was used equally by martial artists, actors, and religious experts.

Doing the Shaolin forms with a group is a strangely empowering feeling—the barriers between people seem to dissolve. The art of Shaolin was practiced in and around temples, particularly Buddhist temples, but not exclusively. Temples were also a place for performing opera. Furthermore, temples played a role in aiding, supporting, and keeping unmarried men occupied. It was widely believed that getting married was an obligation, yet the tight marriage market made it difficult for poor men to marry. By some estimates, 25 percent of men never managed to marry. These men used temple culture as a social base, and most of them were not monks. China had large numbers of orphans, and it was the job of temples to adopt and train them. Opera troops also adopted orphans. But in the popular imagination, traveling opera performers and itinerant monks were part of the unmarried class called "bare-sticks," whose bad behavior was also a source of orphans. In the theater, as in real life, monks can be both heroes and villains.

Meir Shahar's book *Shaolin Monastery* is an excellent source for more information about the origins of Shaolin. In it he shows that the Daoist movement practices called *daoyin* were incorporated into Shaolin martial arts from the beginning. As we explained in the previous section, *daoyin* practices were also incorporated into theatrical training.

Traveling actor monks and traveling Shaolin monks occupied the same space in reality and in people's imagination. In essence, they dressed and acted the same role; they shared disciplined practices, specific skills with the same embedded meanings, and practical techniques.

Conclusion

We have now looked at Chinese martial arts from three different perspectives. First we looked at religion and theater from the point of view of *martial skill.* Then we looked at religion and martial skill from the point of view of *theater.* Finally, we looked at martial skill and theater from the point of view of *religion.* When looking at actual examples, the integration of theater, religion and martial skills becomes easy to see. However, this cultural history of Chinese martial arts is still missing a piece of the puzzle. The next chapter explains how martial arts, which once completely integrated religion, theater and martial skills, came to be seen as distinct realms with only loose connections.

The End of Caste and the Beginning of Commercial Freedom

Opera as Rebellion

One of the reasons Chinese martial arts are hard to see in a historical context is that they went through a double transformation between about 1850 and 1930. In order to understand how modern arts have developed, it is necessary to look back through two profound cultural shifts. Without understanding those two changes it is impossible to reconcile what these arts once were with what they are today. Not only will many core aspects of the arts be misunderstood, but access to them will be lost because accurate explanations of their deep content cannot be grasped without this context. It's not even possible to know what questions to ask.

The first transformation was a change in the way theater and opera were perceived in the popular imagination. Theater, as a central organizing and religious experience, in a sense had to die for the intrinsic rebelliousness of theater to become *real* rebellion.

The second transformation was the National Strengthening movement to purify martial arts by attempting to strip them of all connections to theater and religion.

The Ming dynasty ended and the Qing dynasty began in 1644 when a horse-riding ethnic minority called the Manchu conquered China. The Qing dynasty remained in power until 1911. While ethnic difference between the Manchu minority and the Han majority remained a source of conflict, the Manchu adopted Han values, and large numbers of the Han gentry became loyal to the government. The Manchu rulers required all Han to wear their hair in a queue, a long braid which was a symbolic form of subordination—slaves of the Manchu were at one time tied up at night by their queues. The penalty for not wearing one's hair in a queue was summary execution. The Manchu also instituted new rules for dress, although two groups were exempted from these rules: Daoist priests, who wore their hair in a topknot, and Buddhist monks, who shaved off all of their hair. On the stage, however, opera performers were free to wear hair and costumes that represented the previous eras, as so much of the material they performed was historically themed.

As explained earlier, opera was exceedingly popular and widespread. Perhaps part of its popularity stemmed from an inherent attraction to rebelliousness. Much of its narrative material spiraled around rebels and bandits, fighting men and women, daring and passionate risk-takers who were in the habit of taking matters into their own hands. But part of opera's popular rebelliousness stemmed from the fact that performers wore the dress of the previous era. The popular call of rebellion from 1644 until the twentieth century was "Overthrow the Qing, bring back the Ming." Some of that symbolic rebelliousness may also have stemmed from the fact that actors themselves represented the underdogs, people of the lowest social caste.

The period between 1840 and the end of the Qing dynasty was a period of intense turmoil. In the aftermath of the Opium Wars, China's ports were forced open by Western military powers, and later by Japan. Chinese culture was shaken by Christianity, commerce, and technology which began to influence everything. There were major attempts by the Qing government during this period to institute reforms in the hope of transforming China into a modern nation. The first of these was called the Self-Strengthening Movement. It involved founding schools on the Western model and sending students abroad to study foreign technology and ideas.[57] Many Westerners were involved in re-training portions of the Qing military and in establishing the production of battleships, and arsenals.

But there was also an enormous amount of resistance. Conservatives within the Qing government fought against the reforms and the general population was often opposed to change. The three rebellions discussed below all began in contact zones where the changes were most intense.

I am indebted in the following section to Daphne Pi-Wei Lei, whose book *Operatic China, Staging Chinese Identity across the Pacific*, contributed enormously to my thinking about the origins of martial arts. In her words, "Whether it was about social reform or revolution, political theatre around this time was inevitably concerned with the performance

---

57   Yung Wing was the first Chinese citizen to graduate from Yale, in 1854.

of an ideal Chinese identity. However, in certain extreme cases, theatre became the *real* revolution."[58]

The first revolt was actually called the Opera Rebellion, because it was a collaboration between opera troupes and the Heaven-Earth Society (Tiandihui) more commonly known in English as the Triads. Li Wenmao, a leader of the rebellion and a star of the opera, managed to bring some hundred ships to the battle. Actors fought in costume, and were assigned to battle groups based on their character roles. After taking control of the port of Foshan (in southern China, near Hong Kong), they continued to rule—in costume—as imperial rulers and government officials for two years. When the Qing dynasty finally took back control, the local gentry went on a rampage in the surrounding area, massacring by some estimates as many as a million rebels and rebel sympathizers. Opera was banned for fifteen years in the entire region.

What is the origin of the southern Shaolin Temple, a mysteriously undocumented site many southern martial arts claim as their origin? The Opera Rebels were finally ousted with the siege of Foshan and a massive fire. This event could be key to understanding the mythology of many southern martial-arts styles, many of which claim to have come from monks who escaped the burning the southern Shaolin Temple, even though there is little evidence that a specific Southern Shaolin temple existed (temples, in general, were of course ubiquitous). Other southern martial-arts schools claim northern origins, even though they appear quite a lot like other southern styles.[59] This trend can perhaps be traced to the fact that some opera troupes, during the fifteen-year ban and directly after it, claimed to have northern origins, even though, they were apparently performing in the southern style.[60] Other strategies of subterfuge were noted, like having giant puppets on hand to replace real actors on the stage in the event that a government official showed up at the performance. Also, the fact that dressing in the Ming style itself was a rebellious act suggests that the costumes of Buddhist monks and Daoist priests had a certain implicit feel of rebellion, especially when they appeared on the stage.

One reason the Opera Rebellion is not well known is that it was largely

---

58   Daphne P. Lei, *Operatic China: Staging Chinese Identity Across the Pacific.* New York: Palgrave Macmillan, (2006), p. 133.
59   I am indebted to Ben Judkins, for this speculation in a personal communication. A less speculative approach to the question can be found in, *The Creation of Wing Chun: A Social History of the Southern Chinese Martial Arts,* By Benjamin N. Judkins, Jon Nielson, SUNY Press, 2015.
60   Paulie Zink's lineage, for example.

overshadowed by the massive, nominally Christian, Taiping Rebellion. The Taipings—or Longhairs, as they were often called, because they abolished the injunction to wear one's hair in a queue—set up a rebel state that lasted from 1851 to 1864, controlling almost half of the empire and much of the south, including Nanjing. They also abolished the caste system and encouraged actors to take leadership roles in the new government. Although they formally banned opera, because putting gods on the stage was a form of idol worship, the leadership itself was highly theatrical. Leaders wore imperial costumes confiscated from opera troupes and kept opera performers and musicians in their private entourages. The founder of the Taiping Rebellion was a scholar, Hong Xiuquan, who had failed the imperial exams and become enamored with his own version of Christianity in which he was the brother of Jesus Christ. He had access, through going into trance, to the entire family of Jesus and other Biblical figures like Moses. He drew on them for inspiration and as a source of authority, but his religiosity was mostly built around a Chinese cultural vision. The Heavenly Kingdom of Great Peace (Taiping) considered itself a Chinese Christian kingdom. In Daphne Pi-Wei Lei's words, "Professional theatre of the ordinary type had withered away, but Hong held exclusive rights for a theatre of his own enjoyment; moreover, as he and his lords enjoyed the spotlight of history, they became the *real* theatre." Naturally, the leadership of the Taiping Rebellion employed and acted out popular notions from opera of how an emperor-god should look, because opera was the primary experience the low-caste and peasant followers of the rebellion had of imperial authority.

Though it exerted nearly all of its resources, the Qing dynasty was unable to put down the rebellion, and eventually enlisted the help of Western powers. The eventual death toll of this rebellion was high even by twentieth-century standards, with estimates ranging above 20 million for those years.

The Boxer Rebellion of 1898–1901 was a bloody uprising in northern China against native Christians, foreign missionaries, foreign concessions, and, at times, Qing-dynasty troops. The Boxers dressed in Chinese opera costumes and claimed to be invulnerable to bullets. Using swords, spears, and magic, they took to burning large parts of Beijing, Tianjin, and other cities. The Boxers were finally put down by foreign troops who took the opportunity to demand concessions and loot the imperial palace.

Figure 41. Alliance of Eight Nations occupying Beijing, 1901. Courtesy of Wikimedia.

The Boxers have a place in the imaginations of people all over the world. In the West their rebellion is sometimes thought of as the first "interventionist" war, a conflict predicated on misguided but good intentions. The image of crazy youth possessed by the Monkey King and Guan Gong (the two most common possessing deities), believing their martial-arts rituals made them bulletproof, is a fascinating one.

One source of the conflict with Christians at the village level was that Christians considered opera to be a pagan religion, and refused to contribute funds for putting on operas. Operas were used locally as a vehicle to raise funds for public works, so Christians were refusing to pay what was the equivalent of local taxes.[61] The Boxer Rebellion was a unique event, but its defining characteristics were far from rare. Theatrical presentations were still the most widespread form of religious activity in China. Accounts of trance based forms of conditioning against bladed weapons are found throughout the Qing dynasty. Theatrical possession rituals were also common throughout China. [62]

---

61   There were many other causes of this conflict, from famine to border conflicts to the way Christians took advantage of sanctions negotiated after the Opium Wars that enabled them to bypass the laborious bureaucratic hierarchies and appeal to the court directly; this in turn made them ideal allies for bandits. See Esherick's *The Boxer Uprising*.

62   Cohen, 113–114, 329. Also see Shahar, "Violence in Chinese Religious Traditions," 2013.

While the Boxers were viewed by other Chinese at that time in complex and interesting ways, it is safe to say that belief in their magical powers and martial prowess was widespread. Ideas that connected religious devotion, theatrical characters, magic, and martial arts were not only widely held, they were the stuff daily life was made of. (See appendix 1.)

The Boxers put on extreme theatrical spectacles, asserting Chinese cultural superiority, with the goal of exterminating Westerners, Chinese Christians, and even those who possessed Western things.

> The Boxers...bolstered their popularity among the superstitious populace with magic, with displays of supernatural powers, and most importantly with theatricality. They often performed rituals at night: they could produce fire by simply pointing to the sky; knives and spears could do them no harm. Theatricality operated both within and without theatre— before every uprising, plays were put on in the marketplace to drum up popular support and to encourage the troops, and with costumes, theatrical and mythical characters, and legendary weapons, the troops turned real battles into dramatic play...
>
> All the Boxer performers played familiar historical, fictional, dramatic or religious characters: after the spell was chanted, the Boxers went into a trance, as if possessed by spirits. They then introduced their assumed identities: Women would take on fictional women warrior character roles, such as Fan Lihua and Liu Jinding, while men had a larger repertoire, from national icons like Li Bo (the famous Tang poet) to popular fictional characters such as the Monkey King (Sun Wukong) and Pig (Zhu Bajie) from the popular novel *Journey to the West (Xiyou ji)*.[63]

All three of these rebellions were real military affairs, and all three drew on the movement language of the opera for skill, inspiration, and as a model of the way the world works. Opera blended with rebellion as martial arts, and in a sense, real opera had to die for real rebellion to take its place. The martial arts have always been theatrical and creative, even in a milieu of pervasive violence.

---

63   Daphne P. Lei, *Operatic China*, p. 154-155.

Modernity, Feminism, Christianity, Commerce, and Medicine

While soft, flowing movement is a common characteristic of many Chinese martial arts, and was certainly widespread as a performing skill throughout China, no art is more strongly associated with free-flowing circulation than *taijiquan*. The art's rise to prominence began around 1880, a time when under Christian influence women were being encouraged to stop binding their feet, and if their feet were already bound, to go through a dramatic, long, and painful process of unbinding. It is generally agreed that the majority of women had bound feet, but certain classes and groups did not. The practice of foot-binding came to end over a period of about twenty years. This extraordinary change in Chinese culture was profound and intense. Chinese reformers struggled with feelings of inferiority to Christians and Japanese; they felt they were physically weaker, that the power of their women was literally being confined, that they were failures in commerce, technology, and the free circulation of ideas. These reformers, looking for homegrown sources of pride, happened upon *taijiquan*.

Taijiquan probably came to national fame because it was the perfect metaphor for freeing women from the confines of bound feet.[64] It made use of flowing *qi* and extraordinary circulatory abilities, along with a soft, feminine type of potency, but men took great interest in *taijiquan* too. It became a tool for changing hearts and minds because it could be traditional without being anti-modern. It could promote the notion of female emancipation and empowerment while also giving special privilege to traditional texts, movement, body type, cosmological terminology, and Chinese identity.[65]

Not only was *taijiquan* a Chinese form of exercise, but it recast the notion of "weak" men into men so sensitive and physically disciplined that they could effortlessly defeat stronger opponents. Free-flowing circulation in and around the body matched the notion of free-flowing circulation in the realm of commerce and ideas much better than the strength and endurance types of exercises promoted by Christians. *Taijiquan* was metaphorically superior to the disciplines of the West. It

---

64   This is an incredibly neglected area of Chinese cultural history. The only significant work that the author is aware of was done by Dorothy Ko, *Cinderella's Sisters: A Revisionist History of Footbinding.* University of California Press, 2005.

65   *See* Adam Frank, *Taijiquan and the Search for the Little Old Chinese Man: Understanding Identity Through Martial Arts.* Macmillan, 2006.

was the antidote to the confinement and restriction of foot-binding; it was promoted as a model of how China could transform itself from the inside out.

But the story of the spread of *taijiquan* didn't begin there, and it doesn't end there, either. With the rise and fall of the Boxer Rebellion and the formation of the new Republic in 1912, there was a strong anti-martial arts movement. Martial arts were seen as backwards and silly, full of magical thinking and secrecy. To meet this attack, a movement called the "Pure Martial Arts Society" (Jingwu Hui) fought to establish a middle ground, defending martial arts as traditional exercise that was good for health and could be leveraged to improve the self-image of China as a strong nation.

During this same period, Chinese religion was also labeled backwards and superstitious. In order to survive, it went through complex transformations. One of the ways Daoism rebranded itself was by promoting self-cultivation as central, and diminishing the role of ritual and talismans. Self-cultivation practices—particularly *neidan*, the transformation of the inner elixir in stillness—was recast with anatomically specific language and descriptions of physiology, and attempts were made to make it more transparent and accessible to a constituency.

War, Humiliation, and "Pure" Martial Arts

In the early twentieth century, Chinese people, particularly urban people, were deeply humiliated. For 300 years they had been under foreign Manchu rulers, forced to wear their hair in a queue as symbolic slaves. The Chinese people saw themselves as collaborators in their own oppression. They had been unable to work together to overthrow a weak, corrupt government until a group of nine foreign powers allied to bring China to its knees. All the foreign powers except Japan were Christian, and all were promoters of modernity.[66]

The ideas of science, rationality, feminism, purity of form and function, transparent clarity, and the free circulation of international commerce swept the country like wildfire. China turned on itself. Anything old that required oral transmission; anything mysterious, secret, difficult to learn, or regionally particular was viciously attacked as the cause of China's past failures and humiliations. Thus, it was claimed, martial

---

66   The actual British colonial forces on the ground, however, were not Christians, they were mostly Rajputs from North India.

arts were practiced by "…dirty herbalists, religious nuts, and desperate performers who gather up ignorant crowds and blocked traffic."[67] Prominent Chinese intellectuals of the New Culture Movement,[68] activist and writer Lu Xun among them, saw martial arts as a prime example of everything that was wrong about China. (See appendix 1.) To quote Andrew D. Morris in *Marrow of the Nation*, "Stigmatized as backward, feudal, and superstitious, martial arts in the early Republican period seemed… destined for the garbage bin of history…"[69]

Martial arts were to be replaced by *tiyu* (physical culture) which generally meant Western sports fitness and Olympic-style competitions. Physical education departments opened up in schools all over the country.

Huge swaths of martial arts culture were probably wiped out, never to be seen again. Imagine having spent your life developing an extraordinary spirit fist *(shenquan)* only to be surrounded by ridicule on a national scale. Many martial artists probably chose to take their secrets with them to their graves.

As we have seen, martial arts were permeated with secrets, religion, and theatricality. In order to survive, they would have to purge any connections to enlightenment, opera, low-caste actors, ritual, or magic: everything *yin* had to go.

Those martial artists who successfully resisted the onslaught of hysteria did so in the name of modernity. The first powerful voice for making martial arts *part* of modernity was the Pure Martial Arts Society (Jingwu Hui). They argued that martial arts could be a sport like any other sport, and since all the other sports in physical education departments came from the West, having a sport with Chinese roots would be a great source of pride which would help build the nation. For *gongfu* to be a sport it had to be totally open and accessible to women, with a clear standard curriculum; a health and fitness component free of traditional body cosmology terms like *jing, qi* or *shen*; and be competition-oriented. These "purified" martial arts swept the country. Over a period of about thirty years, the term "pure martial" *(jingwu)* was surpassed in mainland China by the term *guoshu*, literally, "national art," signifying

---

67   Andrew D. Morris. *Marrow of the Nation; A History of Sport and Physical Culture in (2004).* [223–27.]

68   The New Culture Movement sought to transform Chinese culture in the decades of the 1910-1920s. This influential movement was led by classically trained intellectuals, who were anti-Confucian and aggressively forward-looking, feminist, and inclined toward democracy and science.

69   Morris, *Marrow* 2007, p. 223–27.

that practitioners were partisans of the modernizing project. The Guomindang government of Chiang Kai-shek founded Guoshu schools in the areas of the country it controlled, and it used martial competitions, along with academic testing, to select officers in the government and armies. When the Communists took power after 1949, they began using the term *wushu* (martial art) and attempted to make the training into a content-free performance by removing all martial skills. They ridiculed individual martial prowess, which pushed any application of personal power underground. After the Cultural Revolution of 1967–1977, when the evil started to thaw, personal prowess in the martial arts slowly came out of hiding.

Early advocates of purified martial arts argued that in the past there had been a pure fighting art that was corrupted by theater and superstition, but which could now be extricated from the ruins of history by being simplified and mixed with fitness training. There were multiple variations of this argument; for example, it was aggressively argued that martial virtues *(wude)* had been lost and needed to be reasserted. The early twentieth century was also a period when martial artists began making up lineages and publishing teaching manuals. Historically speaking, the idea of "pure" martial arts was complete fantasy, but it was what people wanted—a dramatic change.[70]

Martial arts lineages probably did exist, to some extent, as part of theatrical, Daoist, Buddhist, and family lineages—but they were certainly not "pure." Lineage claims allowed people to pretend they came from a great line of masters dedicated to nothing but martial virtue and pure technique. Concocting lineages allowed people to write religion, rebellion, and performance out of history, thereby separating themselves from those humiliations. In claiming martial purity they were exorcising the taint of low caste that had up until that moment followed professional performing lineages, as well as the *yamen* runners who were servants of government magistrates. By claiming a lineage, martial artists were also renouncing the past, both real and imagined, and were saying, in effect, "Now *this* art, which was unfortunately secret for many generations, is now totally clear and open! Anyone with four limbs and two ears can learn it!"[71]

---

70   Ironically, to the extent that the Jingwu movement became an institution and spread to places like Singapore in the Chinese diaspora, it opened itself to more religious and theatrical community integration (perhaps in imitation of the YMCA movement). Today it is considered a repository for older styles of martial arts. The movement to save martial arts really did save them. See Douglas Farrer, "The Coffee Shop Gods" in *Martial Arts as Embodied Knowledge: Asian Traditions in a Transnational World.* SUNY Press, 2011.

71   Morris, *Marrow*, 223–27.

The exact ways in which this change happened in Chinese society were varied and chaotic. In the south, where secret societies were strong and British Hong Kong was protected, a more creative approach to lineage stories was preserved. Wing Chun, for instance, is often said to have been created by a woman. This is possible, but more likely it came from a crossing-dressing actor who specialized in playing women warriors. After all, there would have been hundreds of people like that around in the aftermath of the Opera Rebellion (1856), and they would have been out of work.[72] Likewise, several southern styles are said to have been invented by a magic animal, like a white crane or a praying mantis. It is more likely that they were created by an animal-role specialist from the opera, as there were hundreds of those, too.

The bumpy road to "purifying" martial arts included a trip to the Olympics:

> Chu Minyi,[73] a minister for the Guomindang, invented "Taijicao" (Taiji Calisthenics) and in 1933 wrote a book called *Tai Chi Calisthenics Instructions and Commands*. "Whereas traditional tai chi was simply too difficult for any but the most dedicated martial artist to master, tai chi calisthenics were pleasingly easy to learn and practice." The exercises could be done in a few minutes, and they used a counting formula like jumping jacks.
>
> Chu's Tai Chi Calisthenics were performed on stage at the 1936 Olympics. Fortunately (or unfortunately), he was a peace activist who supported the Japanese when they invaded. Later he was executed for treason, but not before performing one last *taijquan* set in front of the firing squad.[74]

There were many routes to modernization. Kuo Lien-ying, my first teacher's teacher, was an early student of Wang Xiangzhai (1885–1963), who created *yiquan* by distilling the essence of many different styles. Famous for a newspaper article in which he challenged every martial artist in the country to either fight him or sit down and explain their

---

72   Very few martial-arts practitioners associate their art with opera, but Wing Chun is a special case because some of its online practitioners claim it came from the Red Boat Opera. This obviously supports my thesis.
73   Films of Chu Minyi doing Wu style *taijiquan and using creative exercise apparati*, can now be seen on YouTube.
74   Morris, 2004: 223–27

art in plain language, he advocated discarding forms, performance, philosophy, theory, and religion. Though he was known as a superlative martial artist, all this discarding was not good for continuity. His students tended to go in one of three divergent directions, some promoting standing still as a pure health practice, others single-mindedly pursuing fighting skills, and another group concerned with the ability to knock people over by blasting them with *qi* from a distance. This last practice, called *kongling jin,* or "empty spirit-force" is a wonderful magic trick with religious implications, but when presented in the context of "pure" martial arts, it just seems weird.

Standing still *(zhanzhuang)* was the center of Wang Xiangzhai's *yiquan.* He claimed that it was the secret ingredient, the inner training found in every type of martial art he had encountered. That was a great insight, but Wang's students who focused on standing still as a health practice had an almost militant tendency to exaggerate, describing it as "ancient science," or a panacea.

The categorical splits that happened among Wang Xiangzhai's students are an example of why reestablishing an accurate and authentic history of martial arts would be valuable. The reintegrated version of all these elements is a more complete and satisfying way to practice. The elements that have been discarded—forms, performance, and religion—have potency and meaning. They give context to content. Innovating and discarding are noble projects; but without a connection to an authentic history, they often perpetuate misconceptions and degrade the arts.

Religion and Self-Cultivation

The newly formed republican government in 1912 was anti-opera, anti-martial arts, and anti-traditional religion, because as a combined force, these elements were associated with past and ongoing humiliations of the Chinese people and the Chinese nation. As the new government developed, it found ways to compromise, it found ways to co-opt; it set up new standards and sought ways to leverage reformed traditions to serve the new nation-state.

A Pure Martial Art or a Bunch of Tricks?

Many, if not all, of the martial artists who wrote or promoted martial arts in the early twentieth century argued that their martial arts did not require any magic and were devoid of ritual. If their arts had a performance component, they would willingly strip it out. They claimed their arts were based entirely on science, and rhetorically asked, "How could they be based on anything else and actually work?" There were no secrets, and if there had been, they were going to be revealed now! No more tricky talk! The art would serve the national interest, and the national interest was for the Chinese people to be bound together as a strong nation, like other national powers, but with a unique character and history. China would throw off its image as the "sick man of Asia," and replace it with that of a modern, rational, clear, direct, and forthright man.

National strengthening meant Western-style hospitals and feminism, but it also meant reworking religious traditions in order to extract all magic and ritual, and replacing them with forms of religious expression modeled on Protestant Christianity.[75] The reformers attempted to claim the impulse for these changes came from within, that the sources of a "Chinese modernity" had a long history which was finally coming to fruition.

The new model for religion was defined by charitable organizations, weekly services, the supremacy of the texts themselves over clerical interpretation, educational outreach, and most of all, an attempt to create a participatory lay community.

In this turmoil, a space emerged for self-cultivation in both martial arts and religion, although it remained controversial and was eventually totally suppressed by the Communists after 1949.

Self-cultivation's long association with the literati gave it prestige.[76] New religious organizations promoted self-cultivation as a way to engage lay community members. Self-cultivation was interwoven with scientific-sounding vocabulary, creating reductionist versions of the golden elixir that describe *qi* as an energetic fluid-like substance flowing up the spine to the head and back down to the groin (later styled as

---

75   Perhaps it would be more accurate to say that this was a Christian-secular model developed out of a century-long conflict between the powers of church and state in Europe.

76   Teachers of self-cultivation techniques had some flexibility to cross social barriers. This dates all the way back to the Ming dynasty, when quirky hermits with skills that ranged from things like the ability to live off of insects or exercise like a crab, to esoteric meditation techniques, were shared around in literati circles. These circles had an enthusiasm for retreats in beautiful gardens that mimicked mountain hideaways; they were urban hermits. For more information, see Victoria Cass, *Dangerous Women: Warriors, Grannies, and Geishas of the Ming* (Lanham, MD: Rowman & Littlefield, 1999).

the "micro-cosmic orbit"). Anatomically correct descriptions of *daoyin* relegated what had been a fully formed enlightenment tradition to a form of exercise.

Perhaps I have painted too dark a picture. After all, self-cultivation practices have been resilient. One dedicated practitioner can preserve a solo tradition. But the idea of self-cultivation in theater training was largely abandoned.

The nationalist government, after some debate, settled on the notion that there were five legitimate religions, and that all other expressions of religion were superstitions worthy of suppression.[77] These included reformed versions of Daoism and Buddhism that were free of magic and ritual to fit the new model; Protestant Christianity; Catholicism; and Islam. There were debates about Confucianism, but the authorities decided that it could be classified as secular if it rid itself of rituals and sacrifices, which it proceeded to do.

Opera and Film

In mainland China in the 1920s and 30s, whenever opera or amateur theater crossed a line into religious transcendence, ritual, or magic, it was treated publicly as an offense against the progress of the nation. Reformers, set on transforming China into a modern nation, actively suppressed these traditions. In thematic terms, even portrayals of rebellion, assassination, and corruption were ridiculed as too traditional. Formerly popular women warrior roles (played my men), whose martial prowess came from magic and religious initiation that utilized their taboo *yin* powers, were suppressed for being offensive and superstitious. The gods could no longer be on the stage, especially not martial gods with exorcistic powers. Nor could they be the source of power in the martial arts.[78] (As of this writing, the Communist PRC is still censoring films vigorously. I heard it said, jokingly, that crime films are okay as long as they don't have any crime in them; horror films are okay as long as they aren't frightening; and ghost stories are fine as long as they don't have any ghosts. The film industry will be discussed in detail below.)

---

77   See Vincent Goossaert and David A. Palmer, *The Religious Question in Modern China* (Chicago: University of Chicago Press, 2010).

78   While it is not the subject of this book, as literacy spread, a new genre of kung fu fiction, called *wuxia* literature, burst out of Hong Kong and became popular throughout the Chinese speaking world. At the same time as theater and film were being suppressed, *wuxia* literature was breaking new ground and flirting with taboos, although religion was often treated with contempt.

Theater was hit hard by modernity. While the innovation of having women play female roles created a moment of interest, and the appearance of Western-style amateur "talking theater" *(huaju)* spurred a moment of enthusiasm, the overall trend was a death spiral. Simultaneously, performers who had all belonged to a degraded caste were suddenly liberated. To stay a traditional performer meant hanging on to low-caste taint; even worse, it often meant enduring feelings of being responsible for China's national humiliations. Large numbers of performers just quit.

The most *yin* aspects of theater died out. Magic, open homosexuality and cross-dressing, comic gods, playing the opposite gender in a fighting role, animal roles, exorcists, Daoists, Buddhists, old women and other trickster roles, and anything that involved rolling on the ground disappeared, went abroad, or went underground. Fighting roles in general were banned off and on, showing a kind of schizophrenic confusion as to whether theatricality could exist at all without them. Opera became a tiny fragment of what it once had been, and the reverence for the potency of emptiness within the theater became an empty shell.

But performers who could remake themselves into pure martial artists or self-cultivation teachers, or even both, under the guise of modern scientific health education, carved out a powerful niche. When martial artists declared that there were no tricks, deceptions, or illusions in their art, they were trying desperately to distance themselves from the theater and from religion.

But the sad reality is that the hand is faster than the eye. The basis of martial arts *is* skillful deception; the illusion of doing one thing while actually doing another. Fakes, feints, dodges, setups, patterns, unbalancing, disorienting, misperceiving—these are all tricks that take great time and effort to produce. But they are tricks nonetheless. They rely on the opponent being deceived. Even explosive power, joint locks, or effortless throws—these are all tricks. And these are just the most common ones. *There are real secrets!* How else could a big, strong, fast man be beaten by a small, elegant woman?

And that is really the heart of it. Because they were under threat, practitioners in the Republic stated that martial arts were all open and obvious; that anyone could learn them; that they were based on rational, honest, straightforward knowledge. The martial arts were going to be eliminated if a way was not found to make them sound modern. Without this rhetorically skillful defense, martial arts were perceived as the enemy within.

Before the twentieth century, Chinese martial arts had a wide range of distinct character role types. Comic and trickster roles could be young, old, evil, good, sympathetic, not-so-sympathetic, mysterious, resilient, or fragile. There were happily drunk generals and cruel judges, romantic heroes, warrior princesses, fair maidens, disloyal servants, magical animals who fought on the ground, white cranes, dragons with rainbow whiskers, and, sure, tough guys, too. The dawning of modernity brought a kind of theatrical authoritarianism. Suddenly only the serious, virtuous, and nationally proud martial character type was allowed. It was not so much that martial arts stopped being theatrical as that the possible "roles" one could embody as a martial artist shrank down to one or two.

Thanks to opera-trained stars such as Jackie Chan and Gordon Liu, along with the Shaw Brothers movie studio, some alternative roles survived. The Hong Kong film industry put up a fantastic show of resistance. The fact that the *image* of the humble old man or woman capable of bouncing a young tough around like a beach ball survived at all is a huge credit to the creativity and resourcefulness of the Chinese people. That there are at least still drunken, monkey, and dog fighting styles, and that Daoist and Buddhist martial roles managed to survive in the minds of elders so that they could be recreated in the 1980s, is a huge credit to the passion and resolve of the Chinese people. Daoist martial arts on Mount Wudang, Mount Emei, and other mountains have been reinvented and restored in the last few years, and the current openness to religious lifestyles is a very positive development.

I suspect the karate of Okinawa was once practiced in a more openly theatrical way, having come originally from the Fujian White Crane style, but when it reached mainland Japan in the 1930s it temporarily took on a fascist hue. Shortly afterward, it found its way to occupied Korea and morphed into the high-kicking Tae Kwan Do, with a similarly limiting image of the tough hero's body holding the nation together. In China, where there were once hundreds of styles, many ceased to exist. The pressure to discard everything theatrical or religious was intense. The imposition of toughness, of the strong body making the nation strong, infected every style. Styles which already emphasized this character role type became dominant.

Another way to look at this whole process of modernization is from the point of view of the temple religion that once was. The attacks on martial arts, opera, popular types of ritual theater, cults to martial gods, and superstition in general were all attacks on temple culture and temple religion. The first reformers in the late Qing dynasty took over temples all over the country and turned them into schools for teaching modern subjects. After 1911, when the Christian leader Sun Yat-sen came to power, many more temples were taken over for purposes that served the national interest, like government offices, clinics, or factories. The process continued unabated as the Communists took power in 1949, and by the time of the Cultural Revolution (1967–1977), every single temple had been closed. During the Cultural Revolution, the few remaining monks, nuns, priests, clergy, and hermits were periodically tortured and dragged through the streets.

In recent years, however, there has been an enormously encouraging change in Chinese culture, and the survivors of these purges are now joyously teaching a new generation. Daoism particularly has always been profoundly creative in its capacity to reinvent itself, and now this is on full display. But the link between martial arts and temple culture has mostly been severed.

Opera had to die in order for rebellion to happen, and the pervasive theatricality in martial arts had to be re-imagined as "pure" in order for a new China to happen. The old China had to be discarded; magic and ritual and ground-fighting were part of that old world of fantasy, trickery, secrecy, devotion, enthralling passion, possession, and fear. The *unseen* world of gods and spirits as drivers and maintainers of human institutions had to be discarded—and it had to be replaced with the *seen* world, the modern world.

As a way of tying all these ideas together, let's take a look at modern film stars. As professional opera came under increasing forms of pressure in the new Republic, a continuous stream of talent fled to Hong Kong or tried to make a name for itself abroad. Long Tack Sam is a great example: he belonged to a low-caste performing troupe that specialized in doing tricks with the queue—the long braid that all men were required to wear until after 1911, when it became a symbol of counterrevolution and national humiliation. Long made a name for himself on tour and in New York as a magician and acrobat of unrivaled skill. Similarly, Beijing opera star Mei Lanfang travelled the world receiving praise wherever he went, including from Charlie Chaplin—the most famous performer in the world at the time—Bertolt Brecht, and Konstantin Stanislavsky, a father of modern acting technique. Bruce Lee's father, Lee Hoi-chuen, was a Cantonese opera star who likewise travelled the world to great acclaim, starring in more than eighty films.

The kung-fu film industry actually got its start in Shanghai, but after a ban in the 1930s that censored the art, the film industry picked up and moved en masse to British-protected Hong Kong. Bruce Lee was born into a family of professional opera performers. His nickname growing up was "Can't Sit Still." Now ask yourself, what happens to a kid like that, born into a family where all the aunts, uncles, and probably most of the cousins were all trained ritual-theatrical-martial artists? His family saw his potential and trained him.

But the dominant story is that Bruce Lee learned martial arts from Ip Man, who was himself from a literati family. Lee's formal training lasted only three years, and by most accounts, after the first year fellow classmates wouldn't train with him, so he took private lessons with Ip Man. No one knows why Lee's fellow students wouldn't train with him, but it may have been because he carried the taint of low caste from his opera-performer family.

Bruce Lee got into legal trouble in his late teens for participating in rooftop matched fights, most likely associated with the Triads. In a deal negotiated by his family, he was sent to the United States to live with his aunt. His initial plan was to teach cha-cha dancing, since he was also a superb dancer.

The rest of the story is well known: Lee spread martial arts to the West and starred in a number of unforgettable movies. His legacy inspired the Chinese government to make a film about Shaolin Temple starring Jet Li, which caused massive numbers of Chinese to actually go looking for Shaolin Temple, eventually pressuring the Communist government to rebuild it! The Bruce Lee film *Fists of Fury* is actually titled *Jingwu* (Pure Martial Arts) in Chinese. But it is difficult to grasp the substance of Bruce Lee's story without a bit of historical and cultural context to put it in perspective.

Caravan Guards

Many martial artists claim that their art or their lineage came from caravan guards. As explained earlier, teachers in the early part of the twentieth century had strong incentives to make up such stories; however, it is possible that some of these stories are true. There were indeed caravan guards, and the need for guards with martial prowess was real; rivers and roads were rife with bandits for most of history. Yet it is hard to believe a phenomenon as widespread as martial arts, integrated with religion and theater, arose solely from caravan guards who were likely big guys with quality weapons (these were probably guns after 1850) and good connections, who worked on boats or horses, or doubled as porters. If they were more than just itinerant workers, they would mainly have been concerned with utilizing their social network of other skilled men to ensure safe passage for their clients. Opera performers traveled with valuable silks, slept outside of city gates, and were known for their martial skills. If the theater business wasn't going so well, why not offer protection along the roads your performance company had been using as a touring circuit for generations? Why not leverage martial skills in the transition to modernity? That transition was already in full swing by the 1850s. The disruption of trade routes by large land wars may have made toughness a better prospect for low-caste "mean people" than working as itinerant performers, especially in places where opera was banned. "Caravan guard" was a real job description, but it doesn't explain the origins of martial arts, nor does it justify the claim of "pure" martial arts. Considering the times and the circumstances, it is much more likely that these arts had theatrical and religious origins.[79]

Martial-Arts Manuals

Most martial-arts manuals available today were produced by the "pure" martial arts movement of the twentieth century, and should be understood as documents with a specific political agenda. Some of these manuals claim to have been passed down in secret from antiquity. While such manuals did exist, it must be acknowledged that in normal circumstances people didn't learn quality martial arts from books, but rather from one-on-one training. In the theater, however, secret books that confer martial prowess and extraordinary abilities are a key plot device. Most of the major epics have secret books somewhere in their storylines. Copying theater conventions in this manner was a way of conferring authority, because the average person was getting his ideas about martial prowess from the theater.

There have always been people who say, "Hey, learn martial arts! Don't let the bad guys win." The existence of such statements in a tiny number of popular "penny-books" or literati encyclopedias hardly suggests the existence of a martial art free of theatricality or religious vision. But it does suggest that people at all levels of society were enticed by the possibility of attaining extraordinary martial prowess.

---

79   The patron deity of caravan guards was Nezha, the angry baby god who road around on wind-fire wheels and is strongly associated with the internal martial art *baguazahang*.

There is a book by Qi Jiguang called the *Jixiaoxinshu*, first printed in 1562.[80] Qi is apparently the only general in all of pre-twentieth-century history to suggest in writing that unarmed martial arts might be effective for training soldiers. We could simply say he is the exception that proves the rule and forget about it, except that several different schools of martial arts claim some connection to the arts he describes.

Qi is renowned for fighting the *wokou* (*wokou* is usually translated into English as "Japanese pirates," but most of the pirates were probably in fact Fujianese), who were very good with swords and had an enormous number of boats. The *wokou* were the largest group of pirates ever, numbering around forty thousand by some estimates. They were sometimes led by women, and they had hand-held guns, as well as cannons.

Qi primarily used group fighting strategies rather than unarmed martial-arts forms, to attack the *wokou* when they landed; he was ruthless about imposing execution for soldiers who retreated. He slowly wore the enemy down, succeeding where other generals had failed, partly because he was willing to accept high numbers of casualties among his own troops.

Essentially, Qi felt that unarmed martial-arts training was good for courage and morale. (I think Winston Churchill said the same thing about whiskey.) Qi also felt that the unarmed arts created nimbleness and opened the possibility of skill defeating strength. In any event, chapter 14 of his book, called "Quanjing Jieyao Pian" (Cannon Fist for Attaining Nimbleness), is the only part of his book that deals with unarmed combat training. The text is in the form of a song or poem, which presumably would have made it easier to memorize. He describes the greatness of the arts with explosive kicks and flips like Monkey Style, and credits various masters by name. He then describes thirty-two movements with poetic names which were likely part of popular theatrical culture. For example, he uses the posture name "high pat on a horse" *(tanma)* which is still used in *taijiquan*. *Tanma* means a spy, and the movement used in Chen style *taijiquan* mimes hiding behind a horse and peering over the top of the saddle, then cupping the ear to listen.

Qi Jiguang taught his troops these routines, employing local experts to help with this training, and his success against the *wokou* improved the prestige of martial arts. But he was the exception, not the rule: the

---

80   Clifford M. Gyves. *An English Translation of General QI Jiguang's Quanjing Jieyao Pian.* No. AFIT/CI/CIA-93-082. Air Force Institute of Technology Wright-Patterson AFB OH, 1993.

Figure 42. High Pat on a Horse—Gao Tan Ma—which means "a spy."
Photo: Sarah Halverstadt.

notion that present-day martial arts forms and styles come directly from the military is unfounded.

The sixteenth century, when the Ming dynasty was fighting the *wokou*, was a very important time for the creation of martial arts. Not enough research has been done about this period to say why, but there are enough written descriptions of hand combat from this period to say that something important was happening. A handful of military officers commented on the staff-training techniques of Shaolin Temple, comparing them favorably or unfavorably to combat spear techniques.[81] In fact, Shaolin monks were recruited to fight in several battles at this time, although not in large numbers. All this suggests that the military had an influence on the arts of Shaolin, and that the arts of Shaolin had an influence on military training. Apparently there was enthusiasm about the real-world fighting applications of theatrically infused religious traditions.

Paralleling the use of secret martial-arts manuals in the theater, a few historic manuals were produced which catalog or preserve martial skills; but it does not then follow that these were written about a subject which was "purely" martial in practice. If, in the future, the political situation in China continues to thaw, expect secret manuals from the Qing dynasty which mix talismans, deity invocations, and empowerment rituals with martial skills to come out of hiding, giving a fuller picture of the origins of these arts.[82]

Conclusion

The journey of Chinese modernity has been a rocky one. Without knowing the basic history, it is impossible to understand why Chinese martial artists would choose to present their arts as "pure," free from the taint of theatricality and religiosity.

Now that we understand the context in which martial arts were torn away from religion and theater, we are are in a position to evaluate the wisdom of that decision. In the next chapter I'm going to explore how empowering this knowledge can be.

---

81   Meir Shahar, *The Shaolin Monastery: History, Religion, and the Chinese Martial Arts* (Honolulu: University of Hawai'i Press, 2001).

82   In 2015, at the first conference on Martial Arts Studies in Cardiff, U.K., Eugnio Cohen, a student of Meir Shahar, made a presentation on just such a document from a village near Shaolin Monastery.

Figure 43. Woman Warrior, ~1920. May's Photo, California. From the Wylie Wong collection. Courtesy of the Museum of Performance + Design.

Consequences and Conclusions

This is the first comprehensive attempt at a cultural history of Chinese martial arts. I have drawn on recent cultural histories in anthropology and religious studies to support conclusions which are contrary to the dominant narratives, but match my experience. The perspective of individuals like me who have studied both martial and performance skills at a professional level across multiple cultures is slowly opening up the discussion. Changes are also coming from practitioners of Asian religions, who, like me, are representing the second or third generation of enlightenment transmissions in the West.

The anthropological meaning of the term "culture" had yet to be invented in the 1800s, people were still thinking in terms like barbarian and civilized.[83] Unless readers have themselves experienced profound culture shock, they may find the notion of culture elusive. Sources, from a time when the notion of culture did not yet exist, require extensive interpretation. Readers are invited to look closely at these conclusions and either challenge or contribute to them.

Martial arts did not fare well in China after the Communist revolution (1949). The official art of *wushu* was subject to tight state control. It allowed acrobatics, but martial skills integrated with character or narrative were mostly forbidden. While the government did not achieve total control, the transmission of martial arts had some very thin years. After the Cultural Revolution (1967-77) the opportunities to study martial arts slowly opened up, but the historical narrative of Chinese martial arts reverted firmly to the ideology of the previous era,

---

83   James Clifford, *The Predicament of Culture,* Harvard University Press, 1988

a narrative of purity. This narrative, which asserted that martial arts were devoid of theatricality and religion, was born from a time of fear, humiliation and political repression. Almost all the written histories of Chinese martial arts up to the present day have held tightly to this narrative. Inside China, history is carefully censored. But it is more puzzling why outside of the Mainland, histories of Chinese martial arts have followed a similar line.

The turmoil of the first half of the twentieth century has had more lingering totalitarian influence than is usually acknowledged. Several generations of martial artists lived their entire lives under the sway of the pure-martial arts narrative. There are no strong arguments for sticking to that narrative, it has survived only because it is so often re-asserted.

Improvisation

Looking at the martial arts from a broader cultural view suggests re-thinking how they are taught and practiced.

First of all, martial arts need improvisation. In the midst of violent chaos, strategy may confer an advantage, but the best strategies incorporate spontaneity. Improvisational prowess is the pinnacle of martial arts training. Improvisation is not a normal skill, to the contrary, the capacity to improvise is an outsider skill. It is asocial in the sense that good improvisers conform to social standards by choice, not conditioning. Good improvisers are good liars, good at seduction and persuasion. They are good at telling stories with their bodies. Skill at improvisation is a super power. Before the twentieth century improvisation was fully integrated into Chinese martial arts through ritual theater. Such improvisation skills are one reason theater people were outcastes, and why, when people rose up in rebellion, they looked to the theater for inspiration.

Dance

The integration of martial skills into dance is so widespread worldwide that it may be fair to say it is part of human evolution, a birthright. Yet in some cultures people think of dance and martial skills as being separate (this seems especially true where universal education has taken hold). Cultures which fear dance tend to suppress its martial and improvisational elements and obsess on its sexuality. But dance keeps fighting back. Martial arts, especially when integrated with music, are a form of dance.

In the dance world, everyone develops the skill of learning choreography quickly. A trained dancer can pick up an elaborate martial-arts form in a few days. It is a way of using the mind, a type of kinesthetic mastery, an ability to transform seeing into feeling. Frankly, it is a beginning-level skill, not an intermediate one. Martial artists should stop pussyfooting around and develop this skill (take some dance classes if you need to).

Martial dances thrive on virtuosity, the more flips and spinning kicks, the better. Flips and spins in the air are not a big part of matched fights, because those are about control and domination, but air time is great training for self-defense because when you are losing you want to add as much momentum as possible. Self-defense requires using the whole environment, kicking off of walls and flying over furniture. The arguments against acrobatics and musicality in the martial arts are not only weak, they are *ahistoric*.

Music and Acting

There is a Chinese saying that you need a drum and a gong to defend a village.

Rhythmic drumming is a powerful tool for training martial arts, and there is plenty of reason to suspect that before the twentieth century in China it was fully integrated into the martial arts. We should reclaim that.

Rhythm is one of the strongest links between martial skills and performance. But it is one I have covered sparsely in this book because it has to be felt to be understood. It is key to "finding openings" or "cutting off options," and it is key to making stage combat look real. Rhythm is a big part of dueling too, whether for honor or entertainment.

A characteristic of Chinese opera is that the performers on stage are the conductors. This means there is some space to play with the timing in compositions, places that can be lengthened or shortened. Music was improvised on particular themes. Although actors memorized vast amounts of song lyrics and dialogue, some plays were notated simply by a list of who entered and exited the stage, or by bullet points of the content of each scene pinned up on a post backstage. Sometimes the only text was a novel, used as the basis for working out improvised dialogue, stage action and music. Professional level performance required improvisational skills in multiple realms.

Eighteenth- and nineteenth-century *wuxia* literature actually had the sounds of violence built into the text. The word *suo* was written for a sword cutting the air; *tang* for a kick in the face. Most likely these arose from the sound effects and visual cues that make the complex timing of stage combat possible—percussive rhythms—known in stage combat as *cues* and *naps*.

Rhythm can be used to speed up learning, or to implant movement ideas that can be discovered later. Crossing over into the mystical, it can at times strengthen or dissolve one's sense of self.

Ethics & Art

Etiquette has always been part of martial skills development, because violence always has moral consequences. Only in a fantasy world where we are fighting zombies can we ignore etiquette. We should strive to make our conduct consistent with our values.

Improving the ethics of martial arts is a never ending project, one that requires regular evaluation. Martial arts are heroic. People who practice martial arts should strive to be thought of as part of a cohort that is good and decent. But that doesn't mean we need to be serious all the time. Comic heroes, tricksters, warrior women, spritely elders, and gender non-conformists are all part of our proud tradition.

To be good at stopping evil, one must know how evil thinks. Virtuous students need to practice thinking the way evil and misguided people think. Everything villainous from simple bullying and sexual harassment to kidnapping and psychopathology should be practiced. Martially competent actor training can be an emotionally safe place to learn how evil people think. Re-invigorating Chinese martial arts with theater skills isn't just the fun thing to do, it's the right thing to do.

Because I live in what is probably the safest place on earth, ever, and I developed good de-escalation skills and danger management skills as a teenager, I've had very little experience with violence. As a martial arts teacher that has left me free to explore the outer edges of martial arts as lifestyle and artistic expression. Yet it has been extremely valuable for me to learn from and develop friendships with people who put themselves in violent situations as part of their jobs. Violence professionals have been the best imaginable check on the viability of my interpretations of cultural history. They have been overwhelmingly supportive of my perspective. When violence is your job you don't have the luxury of inefficiency. The resistance to seeing the complete integration of theatricality and martial skills tends to come from people with less than twenty violent experiences, or experiences in a very narrow realm, like working as a bouncer at a college bar where all problems are the result of beer and youthful status displays. Good people with lots of experience using force make use of theatricality and do their best to cultivate stillness. It is part of the job.

Play is one of the most efficient ways of learning. The skills we integrate into games are the easiest skills to access in situations when all hell is breaking loose. Playfulness is serious business for martial arts teachers. Matched fights are a great way to test the expressiveness of one's martial skills, and so is performing before an audience. Serious training needs to incorporate outlets for expression—there are a lot more people practicing martial arts than there are jobs in law enforcement.

Chinese culture has some unconscious baggage we may want to divorce from the arts. Many times I've heard that such and such a teacher was virtuous because he didn't teach for money. That isn't virtue. That is a holdover from a time when taking money made you a low caste "mean person," a *jianmin*. Free classes are great, if a teacher can swing it, but they aren't morally superior. Let's all encourage each other to get rich.

If an art takes many years of devotion to get good at, it is a classical-art tradition. Classical arts passed on one-to-one from teacher to student can accumulate fantastic depth in a few generations. By necessity, martial skills in a dangerous world have to be passed on in a short period of time. If pressing need is the focus of a martial art, it isn't a classical tradition and it shouldn't take long to learn. The distinction is important because both are valuable, but can work against each other. Most people will learn faster and better in a milieu with multiple teachers in which students are encouraged to teach and test each other. It's even better if that milieu is producing some kind of performance, be it virtuosity, dramatic storytelling, or matched fights. But even better is the integration of both types of cultural transmission; classical lineages inside dynamic social milieus. That is how Chinese martial arts developed in the first place.

Be on the look out for holdovers from the caste system in the martial arts world. It is fine to call a teacher "master" as long as you retain your autonomy or responsibility. Back when it was illegal to leave the acting profession, a master really was a master, he was a meal ticket and protection from predators. Total subordination probably made sense. But it doesn't now. On the other hand, if students develop good improvisational theater skills they can have a lot of fun playing out master-servant fight scenes. True fighting for honor no longer exists in our society, but it still makes great theater. As Bruce Lee put it, "You have offended my family and the Shaolin Temple—you must have grown weary of living!"

Meditation

Meditation is part of martial arts training. Schools that don't incorporated it are missing an important element. Standing meditation is a profound treasure that Chinese culture has shared with the world. Integrated with stance training, it simultaneously cultivates the expressiveness of the body, and can be a jumping off point for developing character and mime skills. Whether we frame enlightenment as a goal or a longterm by-product of meditation, it is a key source of Chinese martial arts tradition—not just an option for "spiritual people."

Health

The idea that everyone needs exercise to be healthy has been successfully promoted by the YMCA movement worldwide. That is one reason why the idea that martial arts are good for health was part of the pure-martial arts narrative. Chinese nationalists successfully promoted the idea that martial arts was the traditional way to exercise and be healthy, but the actual story is not so simple.

While there is a historic form of medicine from China, which seems almost modern in its attention to case studies and reproducible outcomes, that medicine was a tiny piece of the healing marketplace before the twentieth century. And only a small part of that medical tradition was focused on movement as therapeutic healing.

On the other hand, there are countless forms of healing massage and bodywork which combine religious ideas of exorcism, astrology, blessings, accumulated merit, and charismatic powers. While acupuncture, moxa, cupping, and herbal medicine certainly existed on their own, they were often prescribed with dedicated acts of merit, cosmological prohibitions, or a talisman to eat, burn, bury, or hang up on a wall or a door.

The notion of *qigong* as a medical strategy for healing via improved circulation or detoxification is a modern one. Movement as healing therapy was certainly an important part of Chinese culture, but it was not separate from performing exorcisms and rituals of purification, or chanting scripture.

Emptiness and exorcism are integrated into the martial arts. Rituals of purification—including elaborate bathing; abstaining from foods, drugs, or sex; or, alternatively, ingesting special ingredients; offering incense; and practicing visualizations, along with movements or chanting scriptures—were far more widespread as forms of healing than anything we would recognize as medical. Qigong masters are largely the inheritors of charismatic rituals that are now bolstered by claims of being "scientific" and "medical."

Hey, if it works, why not? Ten percent of people respond to hypnosis as well or better than they do to medical treatments; if you are one of them, that's a lot cheaper and safer than going to a doctor. I am not knocking ritual, charisma, intuition, or alternative diagnosis. In fact, I recommend them, but let's not describe them as medical or scientific.

In the first chapter we discussed conduct, practices, and precepts as ways of accumulating merit; these were also among the most common methods for achieving healing. A great deal of healing movement can be understood as moral precepts in motion, as a way of repairing our relationships with both the seen world of people and places and the unseen world of ghosts, ancestors, and spirits. Pain and illness, in the modern world, still occupy territory in both the seen and unseen realms.

If my students want to have a conversation about how disciplined practice can help resolve the problems they have, that's easy. But it is going to involve examining the person's demonic conduct (think: you already know it isn't good for you), ending ghostly commitments (think: too weak to follow through on), and then making new commitments-to cultivating a body they trust. In most cases, a commitment to getting more sleep will have more reliable results than the intervention of "medicalized" movement.

I think the cultivation of emptiness results in a lot spontaneous healing. But I'm not going to sell it that way because there is no way of knowing if that is true. The martial arts are full of brilliant healing strategies, and most of them come from the acquired intuition of many years of movement experience.

Sleight of Hand and Misdirection

Trickery, illusion, and magic are integral and honorable parts of the Chinese martial arts. Historically and culturally, the term "qi" sometimes means "magic." In the modern world there are basically two types of magic: the kind people *believe in*, and the kind people watch for entertainment. The kind of magic people *believe in* receives a lot of ridicule—mainly claims that the believers are gullible and that the tricksters are unethical, especially if they make money doing it. But the only thing really elevating the entertainment type of magic above the type of magic people *believe in*, is the assumption that the audience knows it is being tricked. In my humble opinion, if an artist's misdirection skills are good enough to separate gullible people from their money, even with their imperfect consent, I say power to them. Maybe in their next lifetime these audiences will pay closer attention in science class.

Deception is an effective way to get people to do things they might not otherwise be willing to do, that is why it is a key component of military arts. Deception can maximize the effect of force; this is sometimes the case even when the deceiver is herself deceived. Charging into a wall of spears has never been an easy thing to do, but there have always been tricks that made it possible. If we think about martial arts fitting seamlessly into the magic- and ritual-saturated world that was premodern China, mundane things like great body mechanics might be reframed as excellent sleight of hand. After all, how is a smaller, weaker person going to defeat a larger stronger one if they both have all the same information, assumptions, and training practices? By training the use of secrets techniques and deception, that's how! In the words of Spanish magician Arturo de Ascanio, "[S]leight of hand must be so good that…misdirection is not needed, and…misdirection must be so perfect that sleight of hand is superfluous."

Old school-martial arts were a tiger with both fangs and good manners. Martial arts without deception are like a fangless tiger. The further we get from actual experiences of violence, the more likely we are to accept martial arts as an abstract method without a religious and ethical basis, and the less capable we seem to be of seeing the central importance of deceit. The antidote to martial arts tricksters and *qi* magicians is not ridicule, it's better tricks and more confounding illusions.

Ground-fighting

Where is the ground-fighting in Chinese marital arts?

In Chinese cosmology, the ground is *yin*, a form of spiritual pollution. Even today in China it is common to see people in public sitting on a piece of newspaper or a small piece of cloth, symbolically creating a barrier between them and whatever *yin* spirits might want to climb up and invade their body. This tradition seems to have survived modernity because it can be rationalized; after all, a thin barrier might create a bit of insulation against moisture or an obstacle for an insect to climb around.

The project of modernizing the martial arts in the early twentieth century was framed in the common imagination as a process of purification. It was specifically those things which Chinese cosmology defined as *yin* that needed to be purged in order for purification to take place. The martial arts were already on the *yin* side of the scales, so purifying them was a mighty and at times laughable project, a source of irony and ridicule (see appendix 1 for a prime example). Until the Nationalist government hit on the idea of proudly promoting martial arts as a kind of homegrown physical education for self-strengthening, the future of martial arts seemed doomed.

Among subcategories of professional performers, the most *yin* were animal role specialists. Those in this category—some 10 percent of all performers—were experts at performing on the ground. They would draw straws among themselves to see who would have to play the dogs and pigs, the lowest of the low.

One question to consider is whether amateurs (nonprofessional performers and martial artists) learned animal roles for ground-fighting, and whether this was an unusual practice. Monkey King and his sidekick Piggy were common possessing animal deities during the Boxer Rebellion, and this type of practice was widespread. There are also accounts of militia troops and festival performances involving people dressed as tiger troops or tiger demons. Were these mechanisms for getting around the taboo of ground-fighting? Is it possible that various types of *yin* polluting practice were widespread in earlier times but required some sort of ritual or talismanic barrier when performed. If that is true, were these given up during the early twentieth century because they were viewed as impure and polluting? Or had they always been so low-status that few people wanted to learn them?

Ground-fighting may have been relegated to "drunken" styles of training, which were the extra *yin* part of any style. Eight Drunken Immortals and Drunken Monkey are among the most highly theatrical of these. Many such styles were likely purged at the beginning of the twentieth century because they were too *yin*.

The rare animal-role *daoyin* I learned from Paulie Zink requires great flexibility, fluidity, and explosive power: monkey, pig, cat, dog, rabbit, frog, phoenix, dragon, butterfly, cow, crab. This art is a storehouse of superb ground-fighting strategies. Practitioners of Chinese martial arts should claim their impure ground-fighting *yin* roots; or acquire the skills to re-invent them.

Seeing the Whole Art in Context

As we have seen, there is little purity in the history of martial arts. And whatever medical function they provided was tied up in talismans and dedicated merit. We can defend our love of the arts without making up a fake history. Fake history cuts us off from huge swaths of practice, and leads to confusion about purpose, function, and value. Actual history gives us access to parts of the practice we didn't know were there.

The Communist government in Beijing continues to control history and speech. Today, the way in which it imposes false histories is ghostly and weak, but the history of imprisonment, torture, and public humiliation is remembered by many. At this point in time, martial artists and actors in mainland China are now several generations away from being able to pose probing questions to their teachers, because in most cases the teachers themselves had that door closed to them. However, it is never too late to start asking questions, but it will require going outside of lineages and the presumed boarders of knowledge. Very recently, Daoists who survived the twentieth century are setting an example in the ways they have been returning to practice and teaching. Widespread recognition that the destruction of Daoism was both deep and wide has inspired a new spirit of cooperation. What had been secret, or held exclusively within lineages, is now being actively shared. This is an incredibly creative time for Daoism.

Studying history and culture makes the arts more accessible. When we deeply understand an art, and have access to it, we are freed from the rigidity of maintaining tradition. If we want to play the long game and stick to the traditional way of learning, we have much better arguments for doing so. When history and culture are accessible, the student can see where tradition is taking them. But we should be inventing shortcuts too.

The great diversity of martial arts exists because individuals have dedicated themselves to something they love. I realize that, by challenging the dominant narratives about the martial arts, I may upset a few people. The stories we tell matter, but not more than the skills and integrity of the people who practice these arts. There is room in this world for people to have different views. Telling your own stories about the art gives you that power—it is your birthright. Free people will use the arts to express themselves.

The possible meaning, function, purpose, and usage of anything in the martial-arts world is bigger than any one person's perspective. Think in terms of the possibilities. Experiment and imagine—that is the tradition!

Expand the range of characters in your repertoire. Enlightenment means being theatrical and performative, not trapped in a martial arts identity. And what is the point of even mentioning enlightenment if it isn't attainable?

Experiencing failure is essential for knowing your edge and having fun. Failure is the antidote to arrogance. If you are a teacher, get better at demonstrating failure. Don't hang on to status and prestige. Belts and ranks are a head-fake, like most teaching strategies. Improvisation needs to be part of the art, because it undermines established authority and creates respect based on actual conduct and ability. Go ahead and use a talisman—just know you are doing it! Trophies should expire, or be made of paper so you can burn them.

Make fake real, and the real, fake. Find the stories in your art.

People in the martial arts world have inherited a lot of angry ghosts, usually from their teachers or their teacher's teachers. In many cases, the teacher does not know the source of the original anger. Exorcism in not just a weird idea, it is a responsibility—it's up to you to get rid of the angry ghosts.

Today is a great day to be a martial artist.

Appendixes

Appendix 1

The following excerpt by Lu Xun was published in *New Youth*, 1918:

Recently, there have been a fair number of people scattered about who have been energetically promoting boxing. I seem to recall this having happened once before. But at that time the promoters were the Manchu court and high officials, whereas now they are Republican educators—people occupying a quite different place in society. I have no way of telling, as an outsider, whether their goals are the same or different.

These educators have now renamed the old methods "that the Goddess of the Ninth Heaven transmitted to the Yellow Emperor"…"the new martial arts" or "Chinese-style gymnastics" and they make young people practice them. I've heard there are a lot of benefits to be had from them. Two of the more important may be listed here:

(1) They have a physical education function. It's said that when Chinese take instruction in foreign gymnastics it isn't effective; the only thing that works for them is native-style gymnastics (that is, boxing). I would have thought that if one spread one's arms and legs apart and picked up a foreign bronze hammer or wooden club in one's hands, it ought probably to have some "efficacy" as far as one's muscular development was concerned. But it turns out this isn't so! Naturally, therefore, the only course left to them is to switch to learning such tricks as "Wu Song disengaging himself from his manacles." No doubt this is because Chinese are different from

foreigners physiologically.

(2) They have a military function. The Chinese know how to box; the foreigners don't know how to box. So if one day the two meet and start fighting it goes without saying the Chinese will win...The only thing is that nowadays people always use firearms when they fight. Although China "had firearms too in ancient times" it doesn't have them anymore. So if the Chinese don't learn the military art of using rattan shields, how can they protect themselves against firearms? I think—since they don't elaborate on this, this reflects "my own very limited and shallow understanding" —I think that if they keep at it with their boxing they are bound to reach a point where they become "invulnerable to firearms." (I presume by doing exercises to benefit their internal organs?) Boxing was tried once before—in 1900. Unfortunately on that occasion its reputation may be considered to have suffered a decisive setback. We'll see how it fares this time around.

> — Translated by Paul A. Cohen. *History in Three Keys: The Boxers as Event, Experience, and Myth* (New York: Columbia University Press, 1997), 230–31. Used with permission.

Appendix 2

Mrs. Archibald Little

Here is a description of such a display from China in the 1880's by Mrs. Archibald Little:

> Some of us really had been there since 5 a.m.; but not till about 9:30 did the trumpets sound. Then the great green Viceroy's chair with its multitude of bearers appeared through the city gates, forty banner-men all rooped their beautiful silken banners in the wet before him, whilst the army as one man went on its knees. The

Viceroy entered the tribune, and the review began. But that entry could not have been better, if so well done, at Drury Lane. And the rest, too, was excellently staged. There was the usual extraordinary mixture of foreign and native drill—fours about, hollow squares with the cavalry inside, the "thin red lines o' 'eroes," and volley-firing, with, in between, wonderful advances of the banner-men, shaking the long poles, round which their banners were rolled, and shouting defiance at the foe. Then in and out and round about darted the Tigers, in ochre-yellow cotton made almost in the foreign fashion, coatees cut short, and trousers not baggy, and tucked in at the boot, as it seemed, at first glance. Then they turned round, and revealed the tiger stripings on their backs and on their ochre-yellow hoods. They came on with long catlike strides, then leapt, then hid behind shields painted to represent the tiger's open jaws, then strode stealthily again, and went through many cotillion figures, their round painted shields sometimes forming a tent for all the tigers, sometimes a series of ladders. Then for a very long time men singly or in twos danced before the Viceroy, showing their skill with two-pronged forks made to catch the enemies' clothes, and rakes, and what in the end looked like a highly painted japanned table-top. Then suddenly, from opposite corners of the parade-ground, darted wild horsemen, each in fantastic attire and on a dashing pony, representing an attacking force of savages; and the army fired on every side at once. Then the artillery appeared with the most marvelous of cannon, slight and somewhat dragon-shaped, and muzzle-loading of course, requiring to be laboriously wheeled round after each volley, and resting on some strange, outlandish supports, that had puzzled us foreigners much whilst carried round upon the shoulders of what now proved to be the artillery

We all felt somewhat mockingly inclined, we Americans, English, and Japanese, looking on from behind the blinds we so often pushed aside to see better. But the worst of it all was, it was all well done; the men appeared well drilled; and though, as the rain fell more and more, the

Tigers no longer bounded as at first, and even their stride lost somewhat of its stealth in the general slipperiness, yet the heartrending thought to all of us was, the thing was meant to be real. As a spectacle it was so successful! But those poor men down there would march in that style against modern weapons of precision, used in accordance with modern tactics, and of course had *run away*! "Poor old China! Poor old China!" rose like a chorus from the pitiful ones. And we wondered, Did the Viceroy realise what he was looking on at? Did his cheeks burn, as our own did? Or did he really know no better, and think it a fine sight, as it was?

The whole wound up with a display on the part of the archers. Silken-clad young men with official red silk-tasselled caps, and the corners of their long gowns tucked up, followed each by a soldier-servant holding above the heads of the crowd a quiver full of arrows, made their way up to the Viceregal tribune, and shot at a target white and long-shaped with three red bulls-eyes one above the other. Each time they did so a big, very big drum was beaten, and a man sprang forward, and picked up the arrow, holding it very ostentatiously at arm's-length. The theatrical effect again was very good; but as far as we could any of us see not one hit any of the bulls'-eyes, and through opera-glasses the paper surface appeared intact, when the Viceroy got into his chair and went off in much the same state as he had come; only everyone was wet through now, and the poor little boys with the Reeves' feathers looked particularly deplorable. On a rough computation, on this occasion at Chungking five hundred soldiers turned out, three hundred of whom, including forty banner-men, were versed in foreign drill and wore scarlet waistcoats. The others were either tigers or orange-clad.

As to the Viceroy, he must have been used to it; for was he not going round the province from Fu city to Fu city reviewing troops? And did it not always rain? He therefore must be accustomed to the archers' consequent failures. But we wondered somewhat sorrowfully whether we had had the great privilege of assisting at one of the last Viceregal reviews of the kind, one of the last survivals of antediluvian periods. All nations have passed through similar stages, as the Scottish sword-dances, Highland flings, and English beefeaters remind us. Or could it be that China is going to persist in living still longer in the Middle Ages? In the one case—for we Europeans are nothing, if we are not practical—let us at once buy up one of the painted shields, and Tiger uniforms, and too often brandished banners with their tribes of attended bannerets. In the other, let us stand back, and look aside, lest our hearts should be too much torn by pity when the great catastrophe comes, and China meets a foe who follows his thrusts home, and is determined to reap the full fruit of his victories.

—Mrs. Archibald Little. 1901. *Intimate China, The Chinese as I have seen them* (1904), p.287-291.

Figure 44. The 18th Royal Irish Regiment of Foot at the storming of the forts of Amoy, 26 August 1841. Michael Angelo Hayes (artist), James Henry Lynch (lithographer). Courtesy of Wikimedia.

Glossary

baguazhang - an internal martial art based on walking a circle

bianhua - a sudden transformation of character or form, such as the Monkey King changing into 1000 little monkeys to fight Nezha

daoyin - opening and hollowing; a yogic practice; one of five Orthodox Daoist practices

Dayu - the Great Yu, one of the ancient founders of Chinese civilization and the ancestor of all shaman and exorcists

Daoism (Taoism) - a Chinese religious tradition

drop step - an term from boxing, meaning a strike which uses whole body momentum because it is perfectly timed with a step

fengshen - the canonization of a god

fengshui - literally "wind-water." The study of placing and designing structures and spaces so that they are in harmony with the unseen world of the dead.

Guan Gong - the god of war, accounting, and loyalty. He was a real general, whose story is told in the *Three Kingdoms* epic *(see cover image)*.

jia - family, school, lineage, or tradition

jianmin - "mean people" the lowest caste in historic China, below prostitutes and thieves

Jianghu - the land of rivers and lakes; a place where martial prowess is the pivot of morality

jiao - school, religion, teaching, or sect, depending on context

jindan - golden elixir. ***See neidan***.

Jingju - Beijing Opera. ***Jing*** means "the capital" and ***ju*** and ***xi*** both mean performance.

jing, qi, shen - a cosmological structuring of the body moving outward; substance, animation, space; *(see Visualization subchapter)*

Kathak - North Indian Classical Dance, "katha" means to tell stories.

kong - Empty. *See* **xu**

kongling jin - an empty, lively force; usually refers to the ability to move or throw people without touching them

lanshou quan - a rare style of Shaolin, the name suggests parrying like opening a sliding door

lianhuadan - lotus flower elixer. *See* **neidan**

Lion Dances - a popular form of performance, done exclusively by martial artists. Associated historically with exorcism and fundraising for secret societies.

ling - lively, agile, spirit; also a tomb with a corpse in it. The material (substance) which anchors a dead spirit. The capacity to wield unseen forces.

mudra - a magical hand gesture (Sanskrit)

Nezha - the angry baby god, also the Third Prince, and the Lotus Prince; second greatest fighter in the world. A lead character in the epic *Canonization of the Gods*. The guardian of Beijing.

neidan, jindan, luanhuadan - inner elixir, golden elixir, lotus flower elixir; are visualization practices which transform the order of perception/action, and are said to confer immortality *(xian)*.

Pangu - a deity who laid down so that his body could became the landscape of the world.

qigong (chi kung) - a systematized routine for moving *qi*. Qigong fever was a mass movement that swept China in the 80s and early 90s, creating "breathing spaces" for people to spontaneously heal from the wounds of the Cultural Revolution.

shouyin - a magical gesture done with the hand

Song Jiang - Painted-face demon generals who transport and guard the statues of deities while they are on tour or when they go to watch a play. The most common type are called *Bajiajiang* (Eight Generals).

Sun Wukong - The Monkey King; the greatest fighter in all the world; the lead character in the epic *Journey to the West*

taijiquan (Tai Ch'i Ch'uan) - often abbreviated to Tai Chi, an internal martial art

tangki (jitong) - a barefoot trans-medium; a ritual expert who becomes possessed by a particular god

taolu - a martial arts form or routine. ***Duifang taolu*** is a two-person martial arts from or routine.

tuishou - Push Hands, a two person game for integrating martial skills

vajra, dorjé, *jingang* - vajra (Sanskrit), dorjé (Tibetan), *jingang* (Chinese); the concept means thunder, diamond, and the hardest substance. By inference it means truth, reality, supreme martial prowess, and a deity associated with those qualities.

wen - culture; civilized; writing

wu - martial or military

wu - empty/without. *See **xu***.

Wulin - the martial forest; a mythical place where martial prowess rules the day

wushu - a confusing term. In the 1980s it meant Communist government approved competition forms, now it is used generally to mean martial arts, or specifically to mean acrobatic martial arts.

Wu Song - the bandit hero of the epic *Outlaws of the Marsh*

wuxia - knight-errant, also the modern category of martial arts literature

xian - Daoist immortal, transcendent

xu, kong, wu - these terms can all mean emptiness without limits. ***Xu*** is empty like a puppet, ***kong*** is empty like a container, and ***wu*** is empty of meaning—to give just a few examples of the ways these terms are used

Xuanwu - Mysterious Warrior *(see box in Martial Theater as Exorcism, subchapter)*

yamen - a magistrate's office and personnel

yiquan - Intent Fist; martial art developed by Wang Xiangzhai in the 1920s, also called *dacheng quan*

Zhenwu - Perfected Warrior, a high ranking god. *(see box in Martial Theater as Exorcism, sub-chapter)*

Zhengyi - Orthodox Daoism, literally *correct unity*

zuowang - Sitting and Forgetting; one of the five practices of Orthodox Daoism; a from of meditation similar to zazen

Bibliography

Allen, Frank and Zhang, Tina Chunna. *The Whirling Circles of Ba Gua Zhang.* Berkeley: Blue Snake, 2007.

Altenburger, Roland. *The Sword or the Needle: the Female Knight-errant (xia) in Traditional Chinese Narrative.* Vol. 15. Peter Lang, 2009.

Ames, Roger T. *Yuan Dao: Tracing dao to its source.* Ballantine Books, 1998.

Amos, Daniel Miles. *Marginality and the Hero's Art: Martial Artists in Hong Kong and Guangzhou* (Canton). University Microfilms, 1986.

Belyea, Charles, and Steven Tainer. *Dragon's Play: A New Taoist Transmission of the Complete Experience of Human Life.* Great Circle Lifeworks, 1991.

Benedetti, Robert. The *forward* to, *Asian Marital Arts in Actor Training,* edited by Phillip B. Zarrilli. Center for South Asian Studies, Madison: Univ. of Wisconsin, 1993.

Bokenkamp, Stephen R., and Peter S. Nickerson. *Early Daoist Scriptures.* Vol. 1. Univ of California Press, 1997.

Boretz, Avron . *Martial Gods and Magic Swords: The Ritual Production of manhood in Taiwanese Popular Religion.* A dissertation, Cornell University, 1996.

————, *Gods, Ghosts, and Gangsters: Ritual violence, martial arts, and masculinity on the margins of Chinese society.* University of Hawai'i Press, 2011.

Brownell, Susan, and Jeffrey N. Wasserstrom. *Chinese femininities, Chinese masculinities: A reader.* Vol. 4. Univ of California Press, 2002.

Cass, Victoria B. *Dangerous Women: Warriors, Grannies, and Geishas of the Ming.* Rowman & Littlefield Publishers, 1999.

Chan, Margaret. *Ritual is Theater, Theater is Ritual, Tang-ki: Chinese Spirit Medium Worship.* Singapore: SNP International, 2006.

————, "Tangki War Magic: The Virtuality of Spirit Warfare and the Actuality of Peace." *Social Analysis* 58.1 (2014): 25-46.

Chen, Fan Pen Li. *Chinese Shadow Theatre: History, popular religion, and women warriors.* McGill-Queen's Press-MQUP, 2007.

Chen, Nancy N. *Breathing Spaces, Qigong, Psychiatry, and Healing in China.* New York: Columbia, 2003.

Clifford, James. *The Predicament of Culture.* Harvard University Press, 1988.

Cohen, Paul A. *History in Three Keys, The Boxers as Event, Experience, and Myth.* New York: Columbia, 1997.

DeBernardi, Jean. "Ritual Process Reconsidered", in *Secret Societies Reconsidered, Perspectives on the Social History of Modern South China and South East Asia.* Edited by David Ownby and Mary Somers Heidhues. London: M. E. Sharp, Inc., 1993.

Desch-Obi, M. Thomas J. *Fighting for Honor: The History of African Martial Art Traditions in the Atlantic World.* Univ of South Carolina Press, 2008.

Deren, Maya. "Divine Horsemen, The Living Gods of Haiti." (1953).

Esherick, Joseph. *The Origins of the Boxer Uprising.* Univ of California Press, 1988.

Eskildsen, Stephen (2008). "Do Immortals Kill?: The Controversy Surrounding Lü Dongbin." *Journal of Daoist Studies* 1.

Farrer, D. S. "Becoming Animal in the Chinese Martial Arts." *Living Beings: Perspectives on Interspecies Engagements 1* (2013): 145-166.

Farrer, D. S. *Martial Arts as Embodied Knowledge: Asian Traditions in a Transnational World.* SUNY Press, 2011.

Fava, Patrice. Documentary film: "Han Xin's Revenge, A Daoist Mystery." Directed by Patrice Fava. Distribution: CNRS Images (France), 2005.

Fleming, A. M. "The magical life of Long Tack Sam." [Motion picture]. Canada: National Film Board of Canada, (2003).

Frank, Adam. *Taijiquan and the Search for the Little Old Chinese Man: Understanding identity through martial arts.* Macmillan, 2006.

Goossaert, Vincent, and David A. Palmer. *The Religious Question in Modern China.* University of Chicago Press, 2011.

Graff, David Andrew. *Medieval Chinese Warfare, 300-900.* Psychology Press, 2002.

Green, Thomas A. and Joseph R. Svinth. *Martial Arts in the Modern World.* Westport: Praeger, 2003.

Grossman, Lt Col Dave. *On killing.* E-reads/E-rights, 2002.

Gyves, Clifford Michael. "An English translation of General Qi Jiguang's Quanjing Jieyao Pian"(Chapter on the Fist Canon and the Essentials of Nimbleness) from the "Jixiao Xinshu"(New Treatise on Disciplined Service), 1993.

Hansson, Anders. *Chinese Outcasts: Discrimination and Emancipation in Late Imperial China.* Vol. 37. Brill, 1996.

Henning, Stanley E. "Academia encounters the Chinese martial arts." *China Review International* 6.2 (1999): 319-332.

Hsu, Adam. *Long Sword Against the Cold, Cold Sky, Principles and Practice of Traditional Kung Fu.* Santa Cruz: Plum Publications, 2006.

Hsu, Elisabeth. *The Transmission of Chinese Medicine.* Vol. 7. Cambridge University Press, 1999.

Hymes, Robert P. *Way and byway: Taoism, Local Religion, and Models of Divinity in Sung and Modern China.* Berkeley: UC Press, 2002.

Johnson, David G. "Actions speak louder than words: the cultural significance of Chinese ritual opera." *Ritual Opera and Operatic Ritual:"Mu-lien Rescues His Mother" in Chinese Popular Culture* (1989): 1-45.

————, *Spectacle and Sacrifice, the Ritual Foundations of Village Life in North China.* Cambridge, Mass: Harvard University Asia Center, 2009

Johnstone, Keith. *Impro: Improvisation and the Theatre.* New York: Routledge, 1987.

Katz, Paul R. *When Valleys Turned Blood Red: the Ta-pa-ni incident in colonial Taiwan.* University of Hawai'i Press, 2005

Kennedy, Brian and Guo, Elizabeth. *Chinese Martial Arts Training Manuals, A Historical Survey.* Berkeley: North Atlantic, 2005.

Keulemans, Paize. "Listening to the printed martial arts scene: Onomatopoeia and the Qing Dynasty Storyteller's Voice." *Harvard journal of Asiatic studies*(2007): 51-87.

Ko, Dorothy. *Cinderella's Sisters: A Revisionist History of Footbinding.* Univ of California Press, 2005.

Kohn, Livia. *Chinese Healing Exercises: The Tradition of Daoyin.* University of Hawaii Press, 2008.

Kuhn, Philip A. *Soul Stealers, The Chinese Sorcery Scare of 1768.* Cambridge, Mass: Harvard, 1990.

Kuriyama, Shigehisa. *The Expressiveness of the Body and the Divergence of Greek and Chinese Medicine.* New York: Zone Books, 1999.

Lagerwey, John. *Taoist Ritual in Chinese Society and History.* New York: MacMillan, 1987.

———, *China: A Religious State* (Vol. 1). Hong Kong University Press, 2010.

Lei, Daphne Pi-Wei. *Operatic China: Staging Chinese Identity across the Pacific.* Palgrave Macmillan, 2006.

Leung, Ting. *Skills of the Vagabonds.* Hong Kong; Leung Ting Co., 1998.

Little, Mrs. Archibald. *Intimate China, The Chinese as I have seen them.* Philadelphia: J.B. Lippincott Company, 1901.

Little, Stephen, and Shawn Eichman. *Taoism and the Arts of China.* Univ of California Press, 2000.

Liu, Xiu. *Daoist Modern: Innovation, Lay Practice, and the Community of Inner Alchemy in Republican Shanghai* (Vol. 313). Harvard Univ Council on East Asian, 2009.

Mackerras, Colin Patrick. "Theatre and the Taipings." *Modern China* (1976): 473-501.

———, *Peking Opera.* Oxford University Press, USA, 1997.

Meulenbeld, Mark R. E. "Civilized Demons: Ming Thunder Gods from Ritual to Literature" (Doctoral dissertation, Princeton University), 2007.

———, *Demonic Warfare: Daoism, Territorial Networks, and the History of a Ming Novel.* University of Hawai'i Press, 2015.

Miller, Sgt. Rory. *Meditations On Violence, A Comparison of Martial Arts Training & Real World Violence.* Boston: YMAA, 2008.

———, *Conflict Communications.* Boston: YMAA, 2015.

Morelli, Sarah."From Calcutta to California": Negotiations of Movement and Meaning in Kathak Dance. PhD Dissertation. Harvard University: Cambridge, Massachusetts, 2007.

Morris, Andrew D. *Marrow of the Nation, A History of Sport and Physical Culture in Republican China.* Berkeley: UC Press, 2004.

Mroz, Daniel. "From Movement to Action: Martial Arts in the Practice of Devised Physical Theatre," in *Studies in Theatre and Performance.* V29: 2, 2009.

Naquin, Susan. *Millenarian Rebellion in China: The Eight Trigrams Uprising of 1813.* Vol. 108. New Haven: Yale University Press, 1976.

———, *Peking: Temples and City Life, 1400-1900.* Univ of California Press, 2000.

Norbu, Namkhai. *Dream Yoga and the Practice of Natural Light.* Ed. Michael Katz. Ithaca, NY: Snow Lion Publications, 1992.

Ownby, David. "Chinese *Hui* and the Early Modern Social Order: Evidence from Eighteenth-Century Southeast China," in *"Secret Societies" Reconsidered, Perspectives on the Social History of Modern South China and South East Asia.* Edited by David Ownby and Mary Somers Heidhues. London: M. E. Sharp, Inc., 1993.

———, *Falungong and the Future of China.* Oxford: Oxford, 2008.

———, "Approximations of Chinese bandits: perverse rebels, romantic heroes, or frustrated bachelors?." *Chinese femininities/Chinese masculinities: A reader* (2002): 226-251.

Palmer, David A. *Qigong Fever, Body, Science, and Utopia in China.* New York: Columbia, 2007.

Paper, Jordan. *The Spirits Are Drunk, Comparative Approaches to Chinese Religion.* Albany: SUNY, 1995.

Phillips, Scott Park and Daniel Mroz. "Daoyin Reimagined: A Comparison of Three Embodied Traditions," *Journal of Daoist Studies* 9, (2016): 139-158.

Phillips, Scott Park. "Portrait of an American Daoist Charles Belyea / Liu Ming," *Journal of Daosit Studies* 1, (2008): 161-176.

Riley, Jo. *Chinese Theater and the Actor in Performance.* Cambridge: Cambridge University, 1997.

Robinet, Isabelle. *Taoist meditation: the Mao-shan tradition of great purity.* SUNY Press, 1993.

Robinson, David. *Bandits, Eunuchs, and the Son of Heaven, Rebellion and the Economy of Violence in Mid-Ming China.* Honolulu: University of Hawai'i Press, 2001.

Saso, Michael. *The Teachings of Taoist Master Chuang.* New Haven: Yale, 1978.

Schipper, Kristofer. "Taoism: The Story of the Way," *Taoism and the arts of China.* Edited by Little, Stephen, and Shawn Eichman. Berkeley: UC Press, 2000.

———, *The Taoist Body.* Berkeley: UC Press, 1993.

Scott, A. C. "The Performance of Classical Theater," in *Chinese Theater From its Origins to the Present Day,* edited by Colin Mackerras and Elizabeth Wichmann. Honolulu: Univ. of Hawaii, 1983.

———, *The Classical Theatre of China.* Courier Corporation, 1957.

Seaman, Gary. *Journey to the North: An Ethnohistorical Analysis and Annotated Translation of the Chinese Folk Novel Pei-yu Chi.* Univ of California Press, 1987.

Shahar, Meir. *The Shaolin Monastery, History, Religion, and the Chinese Martial Arts.* Honolulu: University of Hawaii Press, 2008.

———, *Crazy Ji: Chinese Religion and Popular Literature.* Vol. 48. Harvard University Press, 1998.

———, and Robert Paul Weller. *Unruly Gods: Divinity and Society in China.* Honolulu: University of Hawaii Press, 1996.

———, "The Lingyin Si Monkey Disciples and the Origins of Sun Wukong." *Harvard Journal of Asiatic Studies* (1992): 193-224.

———, "Violence in Chinese Religious Traditions." *The Oxford Handbook of Religion and Violence* (2013): 183.

———, "Indian Mythology and the Chinese Imagination: Nezha, Nalakubara, and Krisna." *India in the Chinese Imagination: Myth, Religion, and Thought* (2013): 21.

———, "Diamond Body: The Origins of Invulnerability in the Chinese Martial Arts." In Perfect Bodies: *Sports Medicine and Immortality.* Edited by Vivienne Lo. London: British Museum, 2012.

Sommer, Matthew Harvey. *Sex, Law, and Society in Late Imperial China.* Stanford University Press, 2000.

Sutton, Donald S. *Steps of Perfection, Exorcistic Performers and Chinese Religion in Twentieth-Century Taiwan.* Cambridge, Mass: Harvard, 2003.

Swaim, Louis. *Fu Zhongwen, Mastering Yang Style Taijiquan.* Berkeley: North Atlantic, 1999.

Thorpe, Ashley. "Only Joking? The Relationship between the Clown and Percussion in Jingju." *Asian Theatre Journal* 22.2 (2005): 269-292.

Unschuld, Paul U. *What is Medicine? Western and Eastern Approaches to Healing.* Berkeley: UC Press, 2009.

Volpp, Sophie. *Worldly Stage: Theatricality in Seventeenth-Century China.* Harvard University Asia Center, 2011.

Wan, Margaret B. *Green Peony and the Rise of the Chinese Martial Arts Novel.* SUNY Press, 2009.

Ward, Barbara E. "Not merely players: drama, art and ritual in traditional China." *Man,* (1979): 18-39.

———, "The Red Boats of the Canton Delta: A Historical Chapter in the Sociology of Chinese Regional Drama." *Proceedings of International Conference on Sinology,.* 1989.

Wells, Marnix. *Scholar Boxer: Chang Naizhou's Theory of Internal Martial Arts and the Evolution of Taijiquan.* Berkeley: North Atlantic Books, 2005.

Wile, Douglas. *Lost Tai-chi Classics from the Late Ch'ing Dynasty.* Albany: SUNY, 1996.

———, *Tai Chi's Ancestors, The Making of an Internal Art.* New City: Sweet Ch'i Press, 1999.

Wile, Douglas. *Taijiquan and Daoism From Religion to Martial Art and Martial Art to Religion. Journal of Asian Martial Arts* 16 (4) (2007): 8-45.

Yung, Sai-Shing. "Moving body: the interactions between Chinese opera and action cinema." *Hong Kong Connections: Transnational Imagination in Action Cinema.* Vol. 1, by Morris, Meaghan, Siu Leung Li, and Stephen Ching-kiu Chan.. Hong Kong University Press, 2005.

Zhang, Jie and Richard Shapiro. *Liu Bin's Zhuong Gong Bagua Zhang: South District Beijing's Strongly Rooted Style.* Berkeley: Blue Snake, 2008.

Zink, Paulie & Michael Matsuda. *The History of Monkey Kung Fu (Ta Sheng Pek Kwar),* Los Angles; Self-Published, 2002.

Index

Z

Made in the USA
Charleston, SC
12 March 2017